Th(un)Lucky Sperm

TALES OF MY BIZARRE CHILDHOOD

BRETT PREISS

The (un)Lucky Sperm
Copyright © 2020 **by Brett Preiss**

Edited by Beacon Point LLC
Cover design by cutting-edge-studio.com
Layout & formatting by Black Bee Media

ISBN: 978-0-6450428-0-1

Disclaimer

Names have been changed to protect the privacy of individuals. While the story is factual and all information is accurate to the best of the author's memory, the names, besides the author's parents and grandparents, have been changed.

Dedication

This book is dedicated to my husband, Jos.

Thank you for not running away.

And to my parents, thank you for unzipping your genes.

It's always funny until someone gets hurt.
Then it is hilarious.

Bill Hicks

Contents

Part I

Seeds of Fate

It was 1962. Dad had an orgasm while Mum was thinking about her new shoes . . . and so my journey began.

Before I knew it, I was suddenly under pressure to make a decision that would affect the rest of my life: as a sperm, I had to decide to either sink or swim. It was a very hasty decision amidst all the noise and flurry of millions of my competitive spermatozoa friends. I had no idea where I came from, where I was heading, what I would do when I got there, or why I had no arms or legs. I just knew I had to stay afloat, fight the current, and struggle against the tide – themes which, coincidentally, became metaphors for the rest of my life. So I went for it. I made it to the finish line first . . . and as a result, I now have to work every day just to feed myself. How (un)lucky was that?

They say the odds of us being conceived come out to one in four hundred trillion; the fact that we're alive, healthy and able to work from nine to five is literally a miracle. I once heard a Buddhist metaphor that described the amazing probability of this 'miracle': Imagine a lifebuoy thrown into an ocean, and a single turtle living somewhere in all the oceans, swimming around underwater. The chances of my being conceived were the same as the odds of Mr Turtle sticking his head out of the water straight into the middle of that life donut – or the same as the chances of my dad having an orgasm sober.

So when I hit the egg, I was the lucky sperm – or maybe unlucky, depending how my life played out after delivery. It's all a matter of perception. Some people look at life as a glass half-empty. Others see it half-full. Some parents think it's normal to tell their child that if they eat watermelon seeds a tree will grow in their stomach; I think that's absurd. Some people might find collecting toenail clippings fascinating; I find it weird. Some parents think spanking a child is OK; I don't. And when they draw blood, I draw a line.

Speaking of blood, on 20 April – funnily enough, the same day as Hitler's birthday – they pulled me out of my mother's vagina with forceps because she couldn't be bothered to push, cut the only authentic connection I ever had to her, and slapped my ass until I screamed. They wrapped me up in a cheap tea towel and whisked me away to the baby room so my drunk father could try to wave at me. And just in case that wasn't enough trauma, the next morning the very same doctor placed himself between *my* legs and removed my foreskin. Ouch! Why were they clamping my penis and hacking into it with a blade? Apparently this was just so I could 'look like Daddy'. The worst thing is, I didn't get a say in it at all. Mongrels.

It wasn't long before my boozed-up daddy, with the neighbour's tipsy seventeen-year-old daughter under his arm, was at the hospital, standing beside me and my pretty mother. Despite being drained from giving birth and having her lady bits hanging in tatters beneath her, I have no doubt that Mum looked stunning. She always made a point of wearing lippy. Dad bent over and covered me with his beer breath, declaring, 'We're going to call him Bradley.' Mum, feeling quite irked with her drunk husband and merry neighbour, rolled her eyes and turned them back to the television; before the two undesirable guests turned up, she had been watching a western television series starring James Garner as Brett Maverick. Without a second thought, she glared at Bonnie and Clyde beside her bed and declared, 'Nope, he will be called Brett. Now the both of you piss off.'

I can only be thankful she wasn't watching *Lassie*.

Lucky or unlucky, that set the scene for my bizarre childhood.

Part II

From Bratwurst to Broken Hill

I was born in Broken Hill (commonly known as the Silver City), a dusty mining town in the outback region of New South Wales, Australia. It is in the middle of nowhere and can be scorching hot. From there, it takes six hours to drive to civilisation, a city called Adelaide, where you can get a decent glass of wine. If you're really thirsty for serious coffee culture and football, it takes nine hours to Melbourne and thirteen to Sydney. If you drive to my hometown from Sydney, you'll find stretches of road that are so long and straight you could place a brick on the accelerator and take a twenty-minute nap without veering off the road or missing anything in the dry, lifeless landscape of red sand, with its scattered blue saltbush and thirsty mulga and Mallee trees as far as the eye can see. The only thing that might wake you from your snooze would be hitting a red kangaroo. After happily hopping across the land with no particular plan in mind, startled kangaroos usually stop and stand frozen in the middle of the road, curious about the strange machine rocketing towards them. What a way to go. Here's a tip: attach a 'roo bar' – not a place where kangaroos will dance for money, but a very solid metal grill – to the front of your car; that way, the impact will do more damage to the kangaroo than it does to your vehicle.

As long as you don't sleep while you're driving, I highly recommend you put the outback of Australia and Broken Hill on your bucket list to visit someday. They really are extraordinary places.

Like most of the lads in town, I came from mining stock. My dad was a miner, and so was his dad, and his dad's dad; in fact, I could trace my paternal family's tradition of wearing mining boots and swallowing dirt back generations to a mining town called Clausthal-Zellerfeld, in the stunningly lush green hills of Lower Saxony, Germany, in the 1840s. I know jobs came to a complete halt back then with wars and recessions, and my ancestors' shovels finally dug the last mineral left underground. I can't imagine what must have been going through the mind of my great-great-great-granddaddy, Carl Frederick Wilhelm Preiss, in 1850 as he rounded up his wife, Caroline, and their seven kids – very Catholic – to emigrate to Australia. They packed their mining boots, tools, family belongings and some buns as they headed to the port in northern Germany. They endured an excruciating four-month trip on an unhygienic sailing ship called the *Herder* (German for 'shepherd') to Australia. Sadly, they lost a couple of kids along the way, then trekked for days through the hot dusty desert in their heavy woollen European clothes to a mining town that had only just begun. It must have dampened their spirits a little. I would have jumped ship well before that – in Bremen, Cape Town or Adelaide – and had a go at chimney sweeping or catching rats for a living instead. Somebody back in Germany must have lied to them, selling them false promises and tickets to a faraway land of milk and honey. If they had only known . . . !

Regardless, the Preiss family were desperate and on a mission for freedom and a better life. Their German tenacity and self-discipline pushed them on through hard times and misery. After moving around from town to town in South Australia, my ancestors finally travelled inland to a town called Broken Hill. On arrival, they grabbed their shovels and started digging for precious metals. Broken Hill must have sounded like a strange name to them; it still does to a lot of people. However, just like languages, names sound normal when you hear them from birth.

The town was founded in 1883 by a boundary rider called Charles Rasp who had nothing better to do one afternoon than to check the boundary fences of a sheep station. He saw something shining and shimmering in the rocky hills nearby that he thought was tin. Charles took different samples . . . and they proved to be silver, lead and zinc. With that discovery, a group of keen geologists and miners rushed to the area, broke the hill and started mining. The numbers grew rapidly in this remote camp, and the inhabitants were clearly too busy digging to hold a 'Name That Town' competition. Perhaps patience was wearing thin when someone raised the question of a name by the campfire one night, after a hard day's digging for little reward in the blistering heat with nothing but cabbage and dry bread to eat. And then one of the miners lost it, shouting, 'Who cares about the stupid bloody name when we're all broke 'n' ill?' and stormed off to his tent while the rest of them, keen to get back to their beer, thought, 'Yep, that'll do' and agreed on calling the fractured mound Broken Hill.

The miners probably believed it would only be a temporary site, like most towns that arose from the gold rushes of the time, so there was no point losing sweat over its title (after all, they already lost a lot of sweat scooping out the precious metals). But surprisingly, Broken Hill grew into a town, and the orebody proved to be the largest and richest of its kind in the world. How lucky for Charles Rasp that it wasn't overcast that day; he would have missed that twinkling moment, and the Preiss family today would still be eating bratwurst and sauerkraut.

Dad was a driller on the mines. His job was to take the tiny metal cage – jam-packed with miners, lamps and tools – one and a half kilometres down into the earth. Once there, he would often work alone in the hot, dark, stuffy pit with nothing but a lamp on his hard hat and a burning desire to excavate some silver, lead or zinc. He would spend hours boring into the wall, his whole body shaking in time with the massive hydraulic drill. No wonder the guy suffered from migraines. I was (un)lucky enough to go down as an adult to witness the awful conditions my dad worked under. I was shocked. Suddenly, it all became clear to me why Dad would drink his life away, why he was always irritated and violent, and why my childhood had been so bizarre. Working like that day in and day out for years would be enough to send anyone crazy.

Up on the surface Dad, Mum, my three brothers and I were housed in one of the many cheap, quickly built bungalows on Queen Street, very close to the mines. They were very basic housing, freezing in winter and unbearably hot in summer. Since there were only two house designs, every second house was the same shape and made from the same materials. One was a basic rectangular timber-framed house on stumps that raised it from the ground so it wouldn't be eaten by white ants; the other version, with a concrete base, was constructed from a basic timber frame covered in wire mesh with cement sprayed onto it. The inside walls were covered with Masonite, joined together with battens. They were cheaply constructed and looked like it.

As in most mining towns, the people of Broken Hill were not expecting the minerals to last forever, so they built the dwellings accordingly. As a result, our house required ongoing maintenance. Every day when explosives were fired underground at 7 am and 3 pm to prepare the mines for the next shift, the ground rumbled, the house shook and it became a sport spotting the new bits of damage – mostly chunks of cement falling off the outside walls, which didn't make the house look very pretty. The blasts were like small earth tremors, so Mum never bought ornaments for the mantelpiece or shelves; they would only end up as jigsaw puzzles on the ground around 7 am or 3 pm.

Growing up in Queen Street was odd and a constant struggle, not least because my family were also odd and a constant struggle. School was no better, though. The other kids would often tease me with 'What was the street called before you moved into it, Betty?' So hilarious. And, yep – Betty. That was the girly nickname my so-called brothers gave me for not being as macho and tough as they were. The nickname spread and I had to suck it up and live with it. So I gave my brothers the nickname 'bastards', just because they were. I was so unlike my brothers that they insisted I was adopted. I thought that was a bit harsh; I preferred to imagine a bit of a mix-up in the crib room at the hospital, some other family picking up the wrong baby by accident. God knows what they collected. I always had dreams of my 'real' family returning to Broken Hill for a refund on their kid and claiming me, their genuine offspring. It never happened, though. Lucky for some, unlucky for me.

So this sperm had no choice: it was given the family it got and it moved into Queen Street with them. You get what you are given, and I did my best to be me in spite of all the hard knocks, pain and tears. Don't get me wrong – there were many happy 'normal' moments, and I must have laughed once or twice. But these moments were very much overshadowed by the bizarre events that are forever etched in my mind, and soon will be in yours. I consider myself a survivor, and my sense of humour really helped me; it's often the Aussie way. I may not have laughed much at the time when my three brothers buried me up to my neck in sand and skidded their bikes around my head, but I can now. I think humour helps you to cope, and sometimes to forgive and move forward. To me, the events of my childhood are now little more than bizarre anecdotes. I hope you can laugh with me at my misfortunes, see the funny side of it all and respect humour in the face of tragedy.

Part III

Snippets of Memory

1. Caught in the Act

Have you ever wondered why we don't remember being babies? When we're just wee wiggle-bums and bubble-makers, we do recognise and remember who our family members are, to make sure we are safe, fed and bathed. But for some reason we seem to lack episodic memory – details of specific events – until we're about three or four years old. Probably a good thing, really; imagine remembering the sights and smells of your mum's birth canal, the constant reflux over your face and everyone else's clothes, and the taste of your mum's milky boobs. No thanks. I'm glad I can't recall any of that. Those first couple of years were basically spent building my brain, exploring my senses and trying to decode the outback dialect. However, at the age of three or four, as my toddler brain began to bring the scattered pieces together, I developed snippets of memory.

One early memory I have is quite vivid, probably because the incident involved happiness *and* pain; apparently the more senses involved, the stronger the memory. I was about three years old and I was lying on the bright, banana-yellow sofa next to my younger brother, Trevor – named after the actor Trevor Howard. Yes, my mother found it rather challenging to think of names for her little cherubs, so she simply chose the name of an actor or character from whatever she was watching on TV as her waters broke. This seems like a good time to introduce my eldest brother Mick (named after Mickey Rooney from the 1954 film *Drive the Crooked Road*) and my other older brother David (named after David Niven in the 1959 film *Separate Tables*). Bravo, Mum, for originality and lack of any family tradition whatsoever.

I still shudder at the thought of all the other names my brothers and I could have been given, thanks to Hollywood: Bing, Humphrey, Yul, Dick . . . or even Doris.

Back to the living room sofa. Trevor was only a year old and was enjoying his warm bottle of milk while Mum and Dad were busy in the kitchen. I was the third in line of the four boys in the family. (Yes, the middle child; need I say more?) I remember lying there enjoying the TV show – its black and white picture contrasting the Technicolor furniture – but also longing to suck that bottle of warm, delicious milk. I hadn't been weaned off it for very long. I couldn't resist. I pulled the bottle gently out of my brother's mouth and hands, popped it hastily into my own mouth, lay back on the sofa and enjoyed the trickle of something warm down my throat - something I still enjoy today. Warm milk is heaven for a toddler, a pleasure beyond measure. That was until my younger brother's legs began shaking, his fists clenched and his breath started puffing away. This was not a good sign. I turned my head to look at him, the bottle still locked in my mouth, when all of a sudden his face turned red and distorted, like he was about to poop. Instead, he let out a high-pitched scream that didn't quite shatter the front window – though it must have come close – but shattered my eardrums and froze my whole body.

Unfortunately for me, it also ignited my mum and dad, who both dropped whatever they had been doing in the kitchen and came running immediately into the living room.

'What the hell is going on?' shouted Dad.

'Brett's taken Trevor's bottle,' shrieked Mum as she ripped it out of my mouth – with my only tooth still stuck in the teat. She shoved it straight back into my brother's mouth to disable the alarm. 'He needs a bloody good hiding.'

'Little bastard. Get up and come here now!' bellowed Dad.

He yanked me off the sofa and held me dangling in the air by one arm as if he were holding up the biggest fish he ever caught, but with much less pride. My world was spinning and so was I as Dad whacked my petite bottom. I must have blacked out from the pain as I don't remember anything after that. What I do remember, however, is resenting my little brother for making me lose both my tooth and my taste for dairy products. I also learnt one of life's important lessons: be very careful what you put in your mouth.

2. Wroo Wroo

Most toddlers are put to bed with a cuddly teddy bear or a soft bunny rabbit. Children need these things because as humans we desire peace, security and comfort. It is only natural. These warm, furry companions often replace the gentle love and touch of a parent, because parents are busy people. Hugging them mimics human interaction. It has been well researched for hundreds of years that a soft cuddly toy soothes a child's anxiety and provides a lot of health benefits. Putting a child to bed with a cuddly toy can also provide emotional comfort.

Guess what I had? Well . . . I was put to bed with a hard rubber boxing kangaroo called Thumper. Yep. The one on the cover of this book (it's the one on the right). How bizarre is that? What were my parents thinking?

Like all preschoolers, consonants were a challenge for me and I quickly christened it Wroo Wroo instead of 'Kangaroo'. Desperate for emotional comfort, I took Wroo Wroo to bed each night, hugging it tight. Even though I would wake up bruised, it became my comfort toy, my only friend, the transitional object to replace the mother-child bond. I needed that, because Mum's affections had suddenly moved to Trevor, the new kid on the block.

3. Show Pony

Another snippet of memory from those preschool years – this one a lot more pleasant – was the day my Grandpa Jack came to visit us. Jack was my dad's father, a lovely man with a huge pot belly and a constant whiff of alcohol around him. It must have been my birthday, as he arrived with a gift for me. Little did I know then that this gift would not only change my life but also keep me sane among the insane. It was a toddler-sized piano and stool. Not the kind with black stripes painted on white keys; no, this gem was a little black grand piano with real black keys that actually played beside the white ones! My stool was the cutest thing ever. It was black with a bright yellow tasselled fringe all around it. The piano came with a little music book with coloured notes and a card with colours to place over the piano keys.

I took to it like a duck to water. I worked out how to play the first few tunes and impressed my parents with my potential talent. For a short time, I was their little entertainer and show pony whenever visitors turned up. It boosted my fragile self-esteem and it did wonders for my middle-child syndrome.

Part IV

Praying, Playing and Penance

1. Sister Stephen

It wasn't long before I had mastered playing all those tiny tunes, with my right pointer finger, from that little music book that came with my toy piano. It wasn't long, either, before I mastered driving everyone up the wall with my endless renditions of 'Twinkle, Twinkle, Little Star'. Mum, Dad and (especially) Grandpa Jack were all musicians, and they could see I had talent for the piano. They all agreed I would benefit from piano lessons, and they all agreed the neighbours would benefit from hearing some new tunes.

Yes, I was well on my way to becoming a piano star. We needed the money. Money was always at the heart of every decision in our household; I believe the first year's piano tuition fees were a Christmas, Easter and birthday present from Grandpa Jack. Thanks, Pops. You may have had hair growing out of your ears and nose, and the teeth of a serial killer, but I will be forever indebted to you for your faith in me as a budding musician; may you rest in the kind of peace I never allowed the neighbours. Mum and Dad apparently agreed they would continue paying after that if I stuck it out and liked it.

Liked it? Seriously? Even when I had nothing else, at least I had Wroo Wroo and my piano. They were all I needed.

Because we were born Catholics, my parents decided to enrol me for piano lessons at the local convent. I really didn't care at that age. I was up for any new experiences and banging away at the keyboard had me hooked. Not even my piano teacher, Sister Stephen – a little old nun with a dark moustache – could deter me. She wore a habit of heavy black woollen fabric, a long veil draped from her head with a little grey fringe popping out the front, and old black boots that clearly showed her vow of poverty. She must have been in her seventies. She was short and stout, with gigantic, heavy breasts that seemingly caused her slight stoop. At first, I found her really scary and intimidating. After a year of piano lessons, I found her exactly the same.

Although I enjoyed the rapid progress I was making through my first genuine piano book, *Teaching Little Fingers to Play*, I found the piano lessons quite bizarre. I was happy to get out of school early, though. Every Thursday at 2 pm, my mother would come to All Saints Primary School, pick me up and drive me to the convent on Lane Street, overlooking the city. The music rooms were joined to the convent. Each tiny room could only hold one piano, a couple of stools, a small cupboard and a nun. There was always a large crucifix above the piano, with Jesus looking down on me. I often used to look up at Him during the lesson, thinking, *And you thought you had it tough!* We would always start the lesson with prayers, an Our Father followed by three Hail Marys. We would have the torturous lesson, and then end it with a few more Hail Marys and maybe an Act of Contrition. I think I actually spent more time praying than playing.

There were times, especially late in the hot summer afternoons, when Sister Stephen would nod off to sleep from heat exhaustion and boredom. I loved those lessons. While she was snoring away and gasping for breath, I had the freedom to just improvise and compose my own pieces. When her snoring got louder, so did my performance. I used to find the greatest pleasure in ending my composition with the loudest chord ever, shocking her back to life.

'Jesus, Mary and Joseph, what on earth was that?'

'C minor chord, Sister.'

'Mother of Mercy, I almost had a heart attack!'

'Would you like me to play it again, Sister?'

'No! Don't play anything. Keep quiet and say your

prayers.'

'My prayers?'

'Yes! Your prayers! Just pray!'

'Pray? To who?'

'To God, to Jesus, I don't care! Just pray and let me catch my breath.'

'Yes, Sister,' I said. 'I'll pray to Saint Anthony because I lost my tooth yesterday and I need it for the Tooth Fairy.'

'The what?'

'The Tooth Fairy.'

'You believe in the Tooth Fairy?'

'Yes. I believe in the Tooth Fairy . . . and God, and Jesus, and . . .'

'Fine. Now keep quiet.'

She would mumble and grumble, wipe the drool off her chin with her manly handkerchief and return to the lesson.

Some sessions were awkward, even weird. Sometimes I had no idea how a piece of music was meant to sound, so I would ask Sister Stephen to play it for me first. It was like asking a zoo sloth to play a run and tag game: fat chance. And even when she could be bothered showing me, it was painful. She couldn't play for shit. It was like watching a polio victim do the Charleston.

'Thank you, Sister Stephen. That was lovely,' I lied. And to keep her happy, I decided to ask her to play again. I requested the short piece on the opposite page.

'Could you please play this one too, Sister?'

'I just did.'

'Oh, nice. Thanks.'

It didn't sound like it. In fact, it didn't sound like music at all. She played it like a drunk. When she finished, she slowly stood up, held on to the piano for dear life, took one step to the side and plonked herself back onto Satan's throne, totally oblivious to the fact that her dopey performance had done nothing to help me. The woman was delusional.

There was one time when she asked me to play four octaves of a G major scale. No problem – I only had one F sharp to deal with. What I couldn't deal with was her leaning forward every time I reached the top end of the piano and conveniently placing those massive breasts in the way so my hands would have to move them. It was disturbing and gave me nightmares. I told her my arms were too short and always insisted two octaves of any scale was enough.

When she was awake, Sister Stephen was mean, tough and unforgiving. If I made a mistake or didn't hold my hands up properly, she would rap my knuckles with her wooden pointer stick. If she couldn't be bothered picking that up, she would pinch my arms, slap my hands, scream and shout. Most people who met this little old nun would have seen a saint; I saw a killer penguin.

I used to try to get on her good side by showering her with gifts for Easter, Christmas and special saints' days so she would consider me one of her 'favourites'. It never worked. She would snap the offering from me, open her dusty little cupboard in the corner and push it in with all the other bribes students had given her. I gave up trying to get this devil's child to like me. However, I persevered. My lessons were every Thursday at 2:30 pm, which meant missing school Physical Education lessons. Not having the slightest interest in sports, I knew this was a blessing in disguise.

From time to time, Sister Stephen would write nasty notes to my parents about how disappointed she was with my technique and how I needed to practise more. I always dreaded handing those notes over; they felt like death warrants. As Dad read them, I would watch his face change instantly from happy drunk to deranged demon, and before I knew it, he would slap me across the ear.

He would shout, 'Go and practise now, you little bastard! These lessons cost a lot of money!' I was traumatised. It seemed pointless to practise, really, as I couldn't hear anything over the ringing in my ear. For seven years, I would pray in every piano lesson that God would take Sister

Stephen to heaven, but He wouldn't. Either there was no God, or He was punishing me for Dad not paying the tuition fees on time. I was an unlucky sperm to score Sister Stephen as my piano instructor, but lucky to have learnt to play this wonderful instrument that eventually brought so much joy to my life.

2. Birthday Surprise

For the first year of teaching my little fingers to play, we didn't have a piano at home for me to practise on. Not sure how Mum and Dad thought they were going to check my progress. However, I discovered that a neighbour around the corner had a piano. Like us, these neighbours were Catholic, and their daughter Paula was also learning from the nuns. I begged Paula to ask her mum to let me practise on their piano. Paula was a year or two older than me, an only child, adopted and desperate for friends. She seized her opportunity, saying, 'Whenever you use the piano, you have to stay afterwards and play with me until dinner time.' That was my introduction to the world of female manipulation. Her strategy worked, of course, but I didn't mind. It was a win-win situation. I got to play the piano and Paula got to play with me.

Paula's parents were lovely and very welcoming. Their house was huge, modern, and always peaceful. After my practice, Paula's mum would give us that typical Aussie snack: an Anzac biscuit – a chewy, buttery oatmeal cookie with a rich history, and almost a meal in itself when accompanied by a glass of Milo, a delicious chocolate and malt milk drink. We would play 'mums and dads', do stage performances on the bright red concrete verandah, and do all sorts of gymnastics on the front lawn. We would play hopscotch and I Spy, and run and tag each other. Paula was one of the luckiest kids in the neighbourhood as she had a metal 'Slippery Dip' – a slide with a ladder. When the slide finally cooled down from the scorching sun, we would spend hours climbing and sliding down it, either together or head first. Excited by the challenge and risk of racing, crawling and testing our limits, we would sprint up it. So much fun. The excitement would always end with Paula's mum shouting from inside the house, 'Stop running up the slide!' We would try every acrobatic move imaginable and could have easily joined the circus.

Paula's father was the dad I always longed for. He was always joking, laughing and hugging Paula; I can't tell you how many times I wished I could get a big hug from him as well. He was a gentle giant and so kind. It was always on the tip of my tongue to ask, 'Could you adopt me as well, please?' Naturally, that was not going to happen, but Paula's dad did become my sponsor when I made my first Holy Communion. That was close enough to an adoption for me.

After a year of piano lessons, practice and Paula's manipulation, my parents must have been convinced I was taking the lessons seriously, because they took me piano shopping. I suspected Paula's mum probably wanted to reclaim her family and had perhaps hinted strongly to my mum to get me my own piano.

I remember the piano-shopping experience as if it were yesterday. The local music shop was called Hartley Harvey's Music Store. Walking into this store full of beautiful pianos was like stepping into a candy shop. I gasped. My eyes lit up and my heart pounded. I just wanted to run around and play every one of them. There were white baby grands, large black Steinways, upright pianos of all shapes and sizes; I wanted to taste them all, and I did. I knew I couldn't have the Steinway grand because it wouldn't fit in my bedroom, but I found a modern, honey-coloured upright piano that I loved. I sat down and played every tune I could remember from my lesson book, *Teaching Little Fingers to Play*. My face was gleaming and I was glued to that honey-coloured instrument. Hartley Harvey smiled.

Dad interrupted my performance. 'OK, that's enough. Come and see the piano you're getting.' He led me to the back of the shop where all the rejects were and pointed to an old, shabby, ramshackle piano covered in cobwebs with a couple of candle holders sticking out at the front. 'There you go, Brett.' My father was trying to be convincing. 'What do you think of this one? I reckon she's a beauty. She only needs a bit of dusting and tuning, and there you go!' There were keys missing . . . and the ones that were there were as yellow and stained as Hartley Harvey's teeth. I'm sure I saw the same piano on *The Addams Family*. I stared at the crippled creature and cried inside. I looked at Dad in disbelief. He was nodding his head as if to say, 'It's this or nothing, kid.' Now I had a choice: either accept the old wooden wreck or play with Paula for many years. It's not easy being a kid.

There aren't too many positive surprises I can thank my parents for, but this one deserves mentioning. It was my seventh birthday, and as usual Mum had organised a large party. Since my birthday was only a month before my younger brother Trevor's, she would always kill two birds with one stone and save loads of money by combining our birthday celebrations. The party was large; all the neighbours were there, and Trevor had more friends than I did. I was thrilled Paula turned up. We blew out the candles, ate the cake, gobbled the fairy bread and chips, and guzzled soft drinks. We were high as kites on sugar.

Halfway through the festivities, a truck pulled up at the front of the house. Mum shouted, 'Who could that be? I wonder what it is?' All the kids ran outside and gathered around it, liked they did when the garbage truck turned up each week. I stood, half-interested, on the verandah. Four strong men were wheeling out a large object covered in blankets. By its shape, I guessed it was the battered *Addams Family* piano. The men took it inside.

I was on the verge of tears from embarrassment. I wanted to hide or run away, but Dad pushed me forward in front of the crowd, announcing, 'Here, Brett – here's your birthday present.' The dread mounted as they slowly took the blankets off . . . and there before my eyes stood the beautiful honey-coloured piano I loved so much! I couldn't believe my luck. I screamed with joy, and happy tears ran down my face. I slid up onto the matching stool, lifted the piano lid, and gently ran my fingers over the shiny black and white keys. I played every tune I knew, many times. All my birthdays had come at once.

Part V

My Parents

1. Belts, Straps and Tyrants

A tyrant is a person who rules without law, using extreme and cruel methods against both his own people and others. Think about some tyrants through history: Ivan the Terrible, Genghis Khan, Vlad the Impaler . . . and my dad, Kevin.

Dad had a problem. In fact, he had a few. Granted, most of them were generated by copious amounts of alcohol, migraines and working long hours underground in the mine, but you could also throw in a volatile, impulsive and demanding wife. My mother, Shirley, was one very frustrated woman.

Mum was an attractive city girl, never short of dancing partners and admirers; living in downtown Adelaide kept this young social butterfly endlessly entertained. It was fate that one Saturday evening in the early fifties, she bumped into my dad at a local dance. He and his two brothers were having a weekend getaway from their dusty mining town, Broken Hill. In those days it took twelve hours by car on a dirt road to get from the outback mining town to the big city. Getting away for the weekend meant you were spending more time travelling than socialising. And even worse, dad and his brothers made the journey on their motorbikes, which took even longer and must have been really uncomfortable. So they were determined to make the event count – and that meant lots of grog, girls and glory in a very short time.

Mum had a wild weekend with the boys from the bush . . . and got more than she bargained for. She fell pregnant, had a shotgun wedding and ended up moving to Broken Hill. Voilà! The city mouse instantly became a desert rat. It may have been an exciting adventure at first, but once the honeymoon was over and the dust had settled, frustration and resentment got a grip on this city lass.

Dad didn't need a reason to lash out, yell or get angry. It was in his blood. He was a walking bomb. Anything would ignite him, and Mum seemed to have a magic touch for lighting his fuse. I did, too. I could set him off simply by waking up, by walking into a room or by making a noise, but mostly I triggered him just by being me. I had a lot of creative energy but every time I tried to express myself, I got the creativity slapped out of me. It didn't make sense to me why Dad wouldn't support my passions. I discovered many years later that he had learnt the cello as a kid, and he was a closeted poet, too, writing hilarious poetry during his breaks underground in the mines. Maybe he was jealous of my confidence and courage to be my true self in a macho mining town that expected every boy to be a 'real man' – whatever that is. The social expectations of his role as a miner were to be tough, butch, and sporty, to drink and to swear. Fine, but not for me. I wasn't a miner. I was a minor. A kid desperately trying to learn the cha-cha-cha, bake cakes and show the world how amazing he could be.

Mum was a lot more supportive of my passions. Perhaps she saw me as the daughter she always wanted, or she simply saw herself: a trapped cultured soul. For so long, she had been accustomed to looking around and finding no way out. I think in me she saw a possible ticket to freedom. So she taught me everything she knew, from baking cakes to cross-stitching on chequered tablecloths. She even taught me how to tap dance. Mum also nourished every creative desire I revealed. I loved paper dolls and creating clothes for them, so she would buy booklets of them every week from the local newsagent in Patton Street. I wanted to learn to knit, crochet and sew. She would put aside grocery money and save it up to buy me needles, hooks and even a toy sewing machine. I wanted to learn the guitar, to type and to dance; before I knew it, I had a guitar, a typewriter, a kiddie's tuxedo and a wonderful range of Latin American costumes for my ballroom dancing lessons. If not for her, I probably would have been forced to join the local miners, digging for minerals and (God forbid) spending the weekends getting drunk and polishing my football boots. Thanks, Mum.

Having said that, Mum was still a very frustrated woman. It wouldn't take much to irk her, and she would always take it out on Dad, my brothers or me – like the time when I was dancing in the living room around the coffee table to loud music. Mum had a headache and was busy in the kitchen, so she shouted through the door, 'Turn that music down!' But since I was too much in my own world, I didn't hear her at first. She returned to the door a few minutes later and shouted again, 'Brett! Turn that bloody music down. I've got a splitting headache.'

I suddenly noticed Mum, stopped, and screamed, 'I can't hear you, Mum. The music is too loud!' Mum, looking like a bull running towards a toreador, grabbed me and pushed me against the wall with her hand on the top of my head. I tried to escape by wriggling away from her, but she grabbed my hair to stop me. While I pulled away, she pulled on my hair. I turned around in shock and saw Mum standing there with a handful of hair. It looked like she was holding a trophy. I put my hand on my head and shouted, 'My hair!' Mum didn't care. She turned off the stereo and said, 'Go to your room! I've had enough of you.' I ran to my bedroom crying. I couldn't believe she had pulled so much hair out of my head. The good news is hair grows back again. In hindsight, I am glad I wasn't doing a handstand at the time.

Living in this isolated mining town, where married women couldn't work and ninety percent of their day was spent dusting, would send any woman crazy. She was stuck in a male-dominated environment filled with constant drinking, cursing and domestic violence – and that was just at home. But Mum would always look stunning, despite the ugly world around her. Mum and Imelda Marcos, the former First Lady of the Philippines, had a lot in common. They both had lots of clothes, lots of shoes and a nasty streak a mile wide. Much as I loved Imelda's butterfly-sleeved dresses, I felt Mum generally had far better fashion sense.

Mum considered herself to be the First Lady of Queen Street. She would persecute the neighbours for the slightest betrayal; her close friends could expect a lashing if they turned up five minutes late to pick her up for coffee or the Musicians' Club dance on a Friday night. However, it was Mum's addiction to collecting shoes that had her in the same league as Imelda. Actually, at the last count, I think Mum had more. Five huge wardrobes full of them. Dad's footwear, on the other hand (or foot), consisted of three pairs: his work boots, his patent tanned leather shoes and some embarrassing sneakers. Mum was a shoeaholic, and Dad was an alcoholic. He said it was cheaper.

2. The Hose

December, and it was hot. Bloody hot. Summer in my hometown would easily reach 45°C (113°F), and it would stay like that for weeks. With that kind of heat, instinct naturally draws you to water. I was very curious by nature, and as a toddler I was about as predictable as a meth-head on a suburban train. Mum never knew which way I would turn at any given moment or where I would be. I was keen to explore, and the big world seemed exciting. So four-year-old me toddled out to the front lawn, grabbed the hose, and turned it on. Even at that age, I had already learnt the hard way not to touch the first bit of water coming out of a hose in summer. If you didn't wait a minute or two, you would scald yourself and could easily pass out from the pain, as the hose and the water inside were boiling hot. Even dogs and cats ran away and ducked for cover for a few minutes when they heard the garden tap being turned on.

Once it was cool enough, I lifted the hose and started to give the plants some water, as they were screaming of thirst. I was also heating up very quickly under the beating sun, so I lifted the hose, placed my tiny thumb halfway over the opening to create a huge fan of water, and started spraying the water high in the air to shower myself with a refreshing summer rain. Unfortunately, I also sprayed the living room window, which set Mum off like a rocket. She flew outside, screaming, 'Turn that bloody hose off!' Of course, I ignored her; she was just being silly. I was too mesmerised by the sensation of the hot summer sun, the cool droplets on my delicate skin and the lovely rainbows I was creating.

'Brett! Do you want a smack? Turn it off!'

I laughed at her, delirious with joy . . . or heat stroke. Mum quickly grew larger and taller as she moved towards me across the greenish lawn. I suddenly realised she really meant it. However, some evolutionary defence instinct kicked in, and I couldn't resist it. I raised my sword swiftly and squirted her from head to toe. She was mortified. She stood there for a brief moment, looking like a scarecrow. Her pristine bouffant hairdo with the little bow in the front was ruined, her pretty pink dress and matching shoes soaked. The next few moments are blank to me; they say the memory part of the brain often shuts down when you are suffering extreme pain. I think I would have been less bruised had I only aimed at her Sunday frock and not drenched her stunning auburn hair, her pride and joy. It's safe to say she didn't appreciate the wet look.

My summer rain routine ended abruptly. The sun's stinging rays didn't match the stinging sensation my limbs were acquiring from Mum's huge hands. I never went near that hose again. Even today, I find it hard to grab one without expecting some trauma to follow.

3. The Artist Awakens

Our house was a dull-looking bungalow with a white corrugated tin roof and beige cement-rendered walls that matched the lifeless gravel lining the driveway. Dad's man-cave was his corrugated shed in the backyard, full of junk, tools, old paint tins and boxes full of minerals no one cared about. Dangerous red-back spiders lurked in the dark corners. I always feared going in too far for fear of getting lost in there and never returning. Mind you, after the painful hose experience, the thought of a Narnian adventure at the back of the shed, escaping to another world, was rather appealing.

It was a Sunday afternoon, and we had finished the ritual roast lunch. Everyone was in the living room, either snoozing from full tummies and the heat or glued to the TV watching endless hours of cricket. Not for me. To this day, I still cannot understand the fascination of sitting for hours watching this king-of-boredom sport. It is mind-numbingly dull, and it always takes ages before anything happens that is even worth sitting up for. Still, each to his own. Actually, I think cricket was invented so that men had an excuse to do nothing in or around the house. Everyone knows you can't do anything until the game is over – and test matches go on for days.

Anyhow, while the family was slowly being hypnotised into a state of unconsciousness, a surge of creativity came over me. I was exploring Dad's shed and came across some brushes and an old tin of paint. After some recent finger painting at school, I was ready to embark on great artistic endeavours. I looked around. *You know, the house could really do with a coat of paint. This lovely bright red should brighten things up a bit.* I don't know how my little arms managed to carry that four-litre can over to the house and lift it up onto Dad's workbench. I also don't know how I managed to pry the lid off the thing, but I did. Never underestimate the power of creativity or the self-confidence of a six-year-old. The artist within had awoken. I dipped the brush into the bright red soup and began painting. The brush was big and heavy. I only managed five very large strokes on the back wall of the house before deciding that was enough for one day. I stepped back to survey my work. The giant blob of scarlet paint suggested that a massive bird had kamikazed into the wall.

However, I was proud of my creation, and that was all that mattered to me. When I'd finished, I tried washing the paint off my hands at the tap near the back door, but for some reason, it wouldn't come off. I had no idea at that age that this is what happens when you use oil-based paint; to me, paint was just paint. I skipped through the laundry and kitchen, leaving bright red marks on the door handles, and into the living room where everyone still sat half-dead watching the game. I went straight to Mum, held my lovely red hands up in the air and said, 'Look, Mum – the paint won't come off my hands.'

Mum looked at me, curious and confused. 'What paint? Where did you get that? What have you been painting?'

I beamed at her. 'The house!'

She leapt up and grabbed my wrist, preparing to drag me to the back door. 'What the hell have you been up to this time?'

We got outside. As I admired my crimson masterpiece with a big proud smile, Mum's face was turning the same colour as the wall.

'Kevin! You better get out here!' she shrieked.

Dad and my brothers, having heard the alarm, came running outside and gaped at the wall in disbelief. My older brothers, always keen to grab any opportunity to get me into trouble, were shouting out comments to fuel Dad's anger: 'Oh no . . . that's bad, Betty!' 'You have to paint the whole house red now, Dad!' They didn't help.

Fifty years later, standing once more in the back garden looking at that now faded red creation, I saw a memento of my artistic talent as a kid. I could still see the look of disbelief on my parents' faces, as well as my brothers', as they emerged from the back door one by one. However, in all honesty, it was also a huge reminder of the painful belting I got from Dad. He helped me lose my remaining front teeth that day. Fate is a funny thing; how different the smile in that year's school photo would have been had I only grabbed a water-based paint that day.

Today, the house is coloured terracotta. I didn't paint it myself, because I have never touched a paintbrush since that creative ejaculation on the back wall.

4. My Own Designer Label

Apparently, my very talented Grandpa Jack was not only a clever musician but also had a trade as a tailor in his early days. I must have inherited his genes. When I was about eight years old, I was with Mum in my favourite toy store in Argent Street; I think Mum was buying a present for my elder brother's birthday. The shop was a tiny, cute treasure trove with toys covering shelves that stretched from floor to ceiling. The elderly owner always wore a suit and tie and had slick, greasy, combed-back hair. He also had a major limp. What amazed me was his ability to straddle the ladder swiftly up and down to grab the toys in the exalted heights of the top shelf.

While Mum looked around, I spotted a tiny purple toy sewing machine that genuinely worked. I was gobsmacked. Visions of 'Brett's Custom-Made Clothing' flashed across my mind. I knew I had to have it, so I begged and pleaded with Mum to buy it for me. I promised to make her a whole new wardrobe. Perhaps it was the prospect of gaining yet more clothes that swung the argument . . . so in a rare loving moment, she bought it for me. I couldn't wait to get home and thread that needle.

Before we even pulled into the driveway, I had already envisioned a unique design: a new garment for my men's underwear collection. I rushed inside, set up my sewing shop in the corner of my bedroom and started sewing straight away. Trevor, curious, immediately stopped playing with his toy cars to watch my creativity and skilful thread work. I grabbed a pair of my light-blue Y-front briefs and some old white pillowslips Mum didn't want any more. I cut long strips of white fabric, sewed them together and hemmed them to make one long, thick ribbon. I attached it to my briefs and made a loop to go over my head, thus creating the first halter-neck undergarment for boys. It was a one of a kind, but I like to think I was sowing the seeds for

Borat's mankini. I was so proud of it. I quickly popped it on and pulled the suspender-looking loop over my head. The loop and suspender had no function at all; in my youthful opinion, it was purely decorative, a piece of high fashion.

After strutting up and down in front of the mirror a few times to admire my bespoke design, I placed my right hand on my hip, turned around and asked my brother, 'What do you think, Trevor?'

My brother's eyes widened. He looked stunned. He didn't say a word, but slowly bent down to pick up his toy cars – still staring at my creation – then rushed from the room.

For me, it was time to share my innovation with a wider public. I burst into the living room, hand still on my hip, to find them all watching cricket. 'Look, everyone! I made it myself!'

Mum glanced up at me and lied, 'That's nice, dear.' Everyone else ignored me, as their eyes were glued to the telly.

So I decided to strut around the room a bit more, sashaying around everyone as if I were on a catwalk. I paused right in front of the TV screen and struck a pose.

My brothers initially burst out laughing, but they were soon screaming at me to get away from the TV. Dad looked up from his newspaper and yelled, 'Jesus Christ, what the hell are you wearing? Bugger off and get dressed!'

It wasn't quite the applause and praise I was expecting. Perhaps I should have skipped wearing Mum's shoes; they really didn't match. Still, I was proud and couldn't wait to design, sew and model some more of Brett's Made-to-Measure Outfits. I asked Mum, in a whisper, if I could go and model my new halter-neck underwear to the neighbours, but for some reason, she didn't think it was a good idea. She shook her head and whispered back, 'They wouldn't understand.' Maybe she thought they just didn't have any sense of fashion.

Part VI

Brothers, Bullies and Barbarians

1. Stuck in the Middle

I got the short straw. As the third of four siblings – all boys – I suffered from 'middle-child syndrome'. It does exist; it is real and it was not fun. I don't think parents and siblings realise the impact being a middle child has on a kid's personality, esteem and ambition. I don't want to bore you with all the psychology behind it . . . but I will have a good moan about what I experienced and how this unfavourable position in my family shaped my drive for attention today.

We middle kids bemoan our fate: it seems like we are being ignored most of the time and we often grow up resentful of all the parental attention bestowed on the older and younger kids – we are short-shrifted. I always felt like I was the odd one out, until I realised it was actually my family who were odd.

As a child I craved the family spotlight, but I had to fight for attention. Nothing's changed, really; even as an adult, I love an audience. No spotlight is ever bright enough. It really didn't take me long as a kid to realise it was futile trying to get attention from my family, so I just gave up. However, that was a good thing in the long run. I decided to create my own world, do what I desired and praise myself rather than seeking the validation of others. I also decided to seek attention from the outside world and chase it. As a result, I still need attention, but I am also very independent and a survivor.

In theory, Mick, David and Trevor are my three loving brothers, but in reality, a lot of times they were also three brutal bullies. My parents saw them as bambinos; I saw them as barbarians.

Mick, the eldest, was really sporty and had a huge group of mates who often hung out together. He was eight years older than me, and we didn't have that much in common. David was sporty as well, and popular with the girls. His nickname was 'Choppers' because of his large white teeth. I did have more of a bond with my younger brother, Trevor, because we shared a bedroom – me in the top bunk, him in the lower one. I got to know him better than my other brothers as we always chatted, told stories and shared jokes. We played a game where one of us would tap out a current hit tune from the Top 40 on the wooden bed frame and the other would have to guess the song. I was hopeless, but Trevor was a genius at it. Perhaps mine were easy to guess as I was a huge fan of ABBA at the time. I had posters of them on the wall around my part of the bed, and even an ABBA pillowslip. Trevor's posters were of Kiss, David Bowie and Black Sabbath.

There were a lot of sibling wars, but I could never get an ally in any of them. If I gave Trevor a hard time, the older ones would protect the 'baby' of the family and give me a good thumping. If the older brothers picked on me, I had no one to help or defend me. If I ran to Mum and Dad, they would say, 'For Christ's sake, toughen up and fight back, you little sissy.' Brilliant. Thanks for that, Mum and Dad. You did wonders for my self-esteem.

Being sport fanatics, my brothers spent most of their waking life either playing or watching it. They were successful at it, admittedly, and their trophies adorned every nook and cranny of the living room. Their names and photos were continually in the sports section of the local paper, the *Barrier Daily Truth*, and sporting gear and uniforms would continually spill out of their wardrobes and the washing machine.

Dad was very proud of his three sporting heroes. He was determined to make a man of me by throwing me into every sport available in the local community – but I had absolutely no sporting genes in common with my brothers. Every attempt I made to play sports turned into a disaster and left Dad disgruntled and disillusioned. I would certainly give him full marks for his tenacity, but zero for understanding me and my interests.

I believe my brothers' favourite sport, however, was tormenting, teasing and bullying me. If trophies had been awarded for this, Dad would have needed to build a special room with huge glass cabinets to display their achievements.

2. Boxing

To toughen me up, Dad had this dumb idea to send me to boxing lessons with my two older brothers. I was around eight or nine years old. I had been hoping for ballet lessons, but requesting something like that only got me verbal abuse and an arm full of bruises. Initially, I didn't begrudge the boxing lessons because, like most eight-year-olds, I was curious and open to learning new things. Besides, every eight-year-old trusts their parents; Mums and Dads always make their decisions for the benefit of the child, right? Plus, anything had to be better than being at home in that house of horrors. Little did I know how wrong I was. Boxing was horror personified. What a brutal sport.

The lessons were held at the local hall of the Police Citizens Youth Club (PCYC), an organisation which began in 1937 and spread across the country rapidly. Its goal was to empower young sporty people – fair enough, but the actual result was that it tortured kids like me. There were activities and lessons in archery, boxing, dancing, gymnastics and fitness. Why didn't Dad read their brochure and realise gymnastics could toughen me up as well? It's not like they would have put me on the balance beam or made me do floor routines with a stick and a long ribbon. Mind you, had they given me the chance, I would have grabbed at it straight away; I already had the ribbon in my decorative sewing box. But no. Dad, ever the macho man from the rough mining town, enrolled me and my older brothers into boxing lessons.

The coach would spend the first half hour teaching us basic boxing techniques; I didn't mind this because the exercises seemed rather harmless. They included 'elbow down and hands up', or 'face behind gloves, eyes down'. It seemed like painless fun. But the remainder of the lesson was brutal: we had to line up near the ring and take turns to jump in and fight each other. I would be put in the ring wearing boxing gloves that felt like massive bandages – so heavy I couldn't even lift my arms, let alone swing at someone. Then I would be set up with an older, stronger, more experienced kid, the stupid philosophy being that this would help me not only to improve my technique but also to reach my potential quicker. The only problem with this theory was that it didn't work. I spent more time knocked out on my back than actually throwing punches. Most opponents were fairly kind, aware that these were only training sessions. But when they put me in the ring with my brother David – who for some unknown reason had been spreading lies again that I was adopted – he relished the idea of releasing his contempt for me. He achieved this by knocking me out and bruising me black and blue. As it was sport, I couldn't run to Mum to tell him to stop. There was no competition. David was fit, lean and muscular and had dark olive skin with a full head of the bushiest curly brown hair. When he stood up in his swimmers at the local swimming pool, he looked like an Aboriginal hunter. When I stood up in my swimmers, I looked like the prey.

As if going to PCYC twice a week wasn't enough torture, Dad had another bright idea: to set up a boxing ring in the living room so we could practise our boxing between lessons. He would arrange the furniture in a square to keep us locked in and would sit on the side shouting, 'Give him a left hook! Throw a jab! Knock him down!' I found it almost impossible to raise my arms because of the huge heavy gloves, so I spent most of the time running around the 'ring' to avoid getting hit. Of course, these home-boxing sessions were really set up for my brother; Dad saw in David the makings of a prize fighter like Muhammad Ali or Sugar Ray

Robinson, and wanted him to get all the practice he could. We couldn't afford a punching bag, and I guess that's where I came in handy.

3. *Australian Football*

Australian football, better known as 'Aussie Rules' or simply 'footy', is a contact sport played by two teams on a huge grass oval. Players can grab the ball to kick it and tackle each other with their hands. It is a national sport, and there was no escaping it in my hometown. There were football clubs in every corner of Broken Hill, and the whole place would shut down every Saturday afternoon through the winter while everyone took off to support their favourite teams. My family went religiously – not because it was culturally expected (and I use the word 'culturally' very loosely here), but because my two older brothers were playing for the South Football Club, our local team.

Even Mum loved going to the footy. She saw it as an outing and a chance to wear her winter wardrobe. All those freezing hours in the grandstand were spent either shouting her lungs out at the players and umpires or sitting back with her thermos of hot coffee, knitting jumpers and scarves for all the family. Now and then, when I had nothing else to do, I would sit with Mum, watching her knit. I was always mesmerised how she could do it without looking at the needles. The other thing that amazed me was the ladies in the grandstand screaming hysterical obscenities at the umpires if they disagreed with a decision. I certainly learnt a lot of colourful vocabulary in that grandstand. I once witnessed a woman arguing with an elderly guy sitting in front of her; exploding with fury, she raised her knitting needle (dropping all her stitches) and stabbed him between the shoulder blades. Seriously, less blood was spilled in a Roman amphitheatre.

During half-time at these weekly football events, the players would run into the changing rooms to replenish their energy, get a rub-down and endure a good talking-to from their manager or coach. Meanwhile, for entertainment and to keep the spectators' minds off the freezing cold, thirty-six little footballers, aged between five and eight and dressed in red and white striped tops with white shorts and long red socks, just like their daddies, would come running out onto the field for a fifteen-minute game. These kids were known as the 'mosquito fleet'. Not sure why; perhaps it was because they looked like tiny, fast nuisances buzzing all over the football oval. This short half-time game gave budding footballers a chance to get started, get a taste of football fever, get hooked and continue this 'cultural' tradition.

My brothers all started this way . . . and I was up next. I got the red and white football jersey (a 'guernsey'), the white shorts and the studded boots. Before I knew it, I was standing in the middle of the oval ready for my first game. I was eight years old, I had a massive audience and I looked fabulous. I really had no idea what I was doing; I ran when everyone else ran and stood still when everyone else stood still. Most of the time, I was looking for Mum in the grandstand and waving to her.

Apart from freezing my winky off in the shorts, football seemed harmless and rather easy. That was, until someone kicked the football high in the air towards me. I was meant to stretch my arms up above my head, focus, catch the ball, turn gracefully, score a goal for my team and revel in the proud cheers of the spectators. Instead, I raised my head slowly and watched the ball plummeting towards me like a missile. My whole body froze, my arms suddenly refused to function, and my short life flashed before me. The ball hurtled right into my face, knocking me flat on my back. The pain in my face, along with the freezing cold, was excruciating.

As quickly as I was knocked down, I sprung back up to my feet, screaming in pain. Everyone kept on playing but I started running – not towards the ball but right off the field, out of the football grounds and home, crying all the way. Needless to say, I never wore that red and white guernsey ever again (it wasn't my colour anyway). The brand-new football boots never saw my feet again, either. They were swiftly ripped off my feet and given to my younger brother to grow into. It took an eternity for the public shame I had caused the family at the footy to settle down; in fact, it took the rest of the football season, which was about six months.

The family, neighbourhood and local community may have kept my embarrassing football incident alive for months, but I was over it and over football the moment I took my boots off. I always wondered what happened to the rest of my team that day. Did they win? Did they miss me at all? And...what happened to the guy who got stabbed by the knitting needle?

4. Easy Target

It was quite common for households in towns like mine to have BB rifles, commonly called slug guns. These were air rifles that shot very tiny soft lead pellets called slugs. They weren't that lethal unless you shot at very close range, but they could blind you if you got shot in the eye. Most teenagers had them to control pests like rats, or to stun rabbits. However, most kids used them to shoot empty beer cans lined up on the back fence, practising their aim for the day they were old enough to purchase a serious firearm. Fortunately, a law banning guns was introduced in Australia in 1996 after thirty-five innocent people were shot with a semi-automatic weapon in a mass shooting in Tasmania. The crazy shooter must have had a slug gun when he was a teenager.

But this was pre-1996. And my brothers, of course, loved shooting. My cousin Billy, who was sixteen years old at the time – twice my age – came to visit one Christmas holiday from Adelaide. He loved coming to the outback and getting feral with the rest of us. He also enjoyed hitting those empty beer cans with the slug gun. Billy wasn't the best shooter. His hand-eye coordination was poor, and I was always convinced he needed to wear glasses. Most of the slugs he shot either hit the fence or went off into the universe somewhere. The small size of the beer cans frustrated him, so he was on the lookout for a bigger target. Sure enough, my brothers quickly pushed me forward and shouted, 'Here, shoot Betty!'

Billy laughed, but loved the idea. 'Brett, stand back a bit and spread your legs. I'll shoot between them just for fun.'

Basically, he saw me as an easy target, and I wasn't going to argue with a teenager who had a weapon in his hand. I naively thought it could be a fun game with my siblings and cousin; perhaps we could take turns. So, like a magician's assistant, I complied and spread my skinny young legs as far apart as an eight-year-old could, fully confident he would hit the dust between them . . . Nope. He didn't. He shot my leg, and it wasn't fun.

Birds burst out of all the surrounding trees – not from the sound of the gunshot, but from my piercing shriek of pain. While I rolled around on the ground, screaming in agony, clutching my bleeding shin, my brothers were screaming with laughter. I even heard one of them shout, 'Shoot him while he's down!' Who needs enemies when you have that kind of brotherly love? No one rushed to help; they simply moved to the back fence to line up the cans for another round. I crawled inside the house with blood dripping down my leg, seeking Mum, the nurse, to patch me up. To this day, I have a scar on my leg as a souvenir from that incident . . . and I still think Billy needed glasses. I also still get very anxious when anyone asks me to spread my legs.

Part VII
First Kiss

Since the dawn of time, people have argued and discussed whether interest in the same sex is biological, environmental, or an issue of mind over matter. It could possibly be a result of all three; however, I am convinced it's biological and genetic. At what point does one become gay –or straight, for that matter? Does it happen with the first thought, or is it only defined by a sexual act? Can you go through life never having a sexual experience and say you are gay, lesbian or straight?

As far back as I can remember, I have always had a strong attraction to and interest in the same sex. Even as a child, I knew I was different. I don't mean because I played with dolls, played dress-up with my Mum's clothes, or learnt ballroom dancing; I really don't believe any of these kinds of activities can 'turn' you homosexual. What I mean is that I had a real physical attraction to people of the same sex.

I can trace being attracted to men as far back as being seven or eight years old. I guess at that age it couldn't have been a 'sexual' attraction, but was more a desire to be close to them, to be given some loving attention or a firm hug, something that was in very short supply from my parents. The only time *their* hands ever reached out to me was to give me a good slap.

It was never an attraction to boys of my own age. They were merely irritating, and I never seemed to have anything in common with them. But there was a myriad of fantasies swirling around in my mind involving the warm, funny, physically attractive male adults in my life – such as Father Vincent, the young local priest newly attached to our primary school. He conducted the Friday morning masses and forgave our weekly sins. I adored him more than God, because Father Vincent was real and he was warm, kind and always smiling. He was very tall, with wavy brown hair, and wore a long white robe; had he only worn a loincloth instead, he would have looked like Jesus incarnate walking around the playground during recess. All the children would run up to him as if he were a celebrity, but instead of asking for his autograph, they would beg him to bless their football or Barbie doll. I was happy just to walk alongside this tall holy man, chat about nothing and wait for his huge hand to gently pat my head goodbye when the bell rang. I was desperate for his affection.

Then there was Mr Gibb, who was the coach of my basketball team, the Pickled Onions. He too was a strong, yet gentle and kind guy who was forever praising us and telling us jokes. I guess I used to fantasise that both these men were my dad because they were so loving, kind and happy – unlike my real, miserable, drunken, bad-tempered father, who used to see me more as a burden than as his offspring.

However, I think one of the real confirming points that steered me more towards men than women was my first kiss with a girl. It was traumatic, and I still shudder when I think about it.

I was seven years old when I befriended a girl called Monica, who lived down the road. She was one year younger than me. We used to play together quite often, and we were particularly fond of imaginary play. We were great performers; role playing as nurses, teachers and families was our specialty. I guess all that practice playing teacher to all the kids in the street paid off later, when I embarked on teaching as a career. Looking back, it's interesting that when we played 'families' or 'school', I always insisted on being the mother or teacher. I guess it was the only time I felt like I had control.

One day I asked Monica to play with me in the regeneration area, a vast nature reserve behind our houses that we nicknamed the 'Regen' for short. It had lots of eucalyptus trees, shrubs and massive mounds of dirt called skip dumps, formed from the leftover dirt from the silver, lead and zinc mines. It also had wild rabbits and the occasional snake.

After we'd been chasing each other around for some time, I grabbed Monica and held her down on the ground. 'Kiss me!'

I really don't know what came over me. It certainly wasn't a conscious choice; I think my first evolutionary sexual hormone just kicked in.

Monica resisted, shouting, 'No! No! No!'

I kept insisting, 'Yes! Yes! Yes!'

The more I insisted she kiss me, the angrier she became, throwing her head from left to right to avoid my pouting lips. 'Stop it! Stop it!'

I was determined to get my first kiss. 'Keep still, Monica!'

'No! Get off me!'

I pushed my face closer to hers. I demanded again that she'd kiss me when suddenly there was a hand on my shoulder and a very loud woman's voice shouting in my ear.

'No, she won't!'

I nearly died of shock. I turned my head and there was Monica's mother, Mrs Jenkins, hovering over me like a rescue helicopter, rage in her eyes and veins pulsating at her temples.

Where the hell had she come from? Did she fall out of the sky? Was she stalking us? Whatever the answer, she now grabbed me by the scruff of the neck and pulled me off her daughter, my left ear still ringing. She then grabbed Monica in turn. Closer to the girl's face than I had ever managed to get, she yelled, 'I don't want to see you play with this little shit ever again, you hear me?' Her voice was so loud and piercing that dogs at the other side of town were barking as she dragged Monica home by one arm.

I stood there, shaking all over, with a pierced eardrum and deflated ego. I didn't get my kiss. But I did get wet pants.

I was in such shock, I had peed myself. Usually a boy's first kiss is a treasured memory; mine was terrifying (well, the attempt anyway). I trudged home, shattered, damp and very confused about girls. I still am.

Part VIII

The Painful Ring

Regardless of my attempts to kiss my childhood sweetheart, Monica, and despite her mother scolding me until my eardrums bled, we remained friends and had regular play dates . . . until one incident sadly put an end to this friendship once and for all.

I was playing at Monica's house one Saturday afternoon at the beginning of the Christmas holidays. She lived across from us, at 11 Queen Street, we were at number 6 (which my strict Catholic upbringing later taught me has a significant meaning: apparently in the Bible, six symbolises human weakness, the evils of Satan and the manifestation of sin. How ironic is that?). Monica's mum and dad were out for the afternoon, drinking at the Union Hotel – one of the forty-two pubs in this town of 30,000 people. Drinking was one of the major sports in Broken Hill. Anyhow, Monica and I decided to head to her parents' bedroom to hunt for props from the grown-up world to help our game of Mummies and Daddies feel more real. Parents' bedrooms are like a forbidden territory, an unknown cave full of curiosity. There is always an element of fear as you delve into the drawers and cupboards. You're so curious and excited at what you might find, but at the same time, you are filled with a cliff-edge terror that you might be caught in the act.

After shuffling through everything, Monica and I tried our best to return everything to the way it had been, to ensure no one would suspect we had been in there. But really, we were amateur felons. We were like a couple of puppies ripping through cushions, throwing fluff and dog hair everywhere, then staring sheepishly at their owner with a look of, 'Mess? What mess? It wasn't us! How dare you?'

After trying on clothes and re-enacting scenes from

the adult world, we veered towards the dressing table to adorn ourselves with makeup and jewellery. What were we thinking? In hindsight, it's clear that kids mostly live in the present, controlled only by their senses – except for common sense and any sense of consequence. I opened a jewellery box and saw a beautiful ring glistening before my eyes.

'Wow, that is such a beautiful ring!' I said. 'Can I try it on?'

Monica swiftly placed it on my finger. 'Let's get married.'

I mean, who could refuse such a proposal? It was all a game and so much fun. I remember enjoying the moment and dancing around the room with my new seven-year-old spouse. Because the ring was so big, it would have fitted on my big toe. I put it in my pocket so as not to drop it and lose it.

Kids get bored and distracted easily. We decided to head outside, so we cleaned up the crime scene and went out to play on the front lawn. My next memory is getting undressed for bed at home and discovering I still had the ring in my pocket! I placed it under my pillow for safekeeping while I formulated a plan.

The next morning was Sunday, and a very hot one. The usual summer Sunday activity was to grab the towels and swimmers and head to the local pool. I would spend the entire day there. On this particular Sunday, something told me to take the ring and marry someone at the pool.

It wasn't long before I saw Sarah, a granddaughter of my next-door neighbour, Mrs Richards. Sarah was a familiar face, around the same age as me and very pretty. I rushed up to her.

'Hi, Sarah.'

'Hi, Brett. Fancy a swim?'

I decided to offer her the ring as a kind gesture, a gift to secure our friendship. 'Yeah, I will – but I have a present for you.'

'Oh? What is it?'

'It's a ring. Would you like it?'

'Wow, it's sparkly! Yes please! Where did you get it?'

I hesitated . . . then blurted out, 'I found it on my way to the pool.'

I remember her eyes widening, her jaw dropping and her red polka-dot bikini strap falling off her shoulder as she stretched her hand out to admire the sparkling diamond now adorning her tiny finger. For me, handing the ring over to her was really a matter of passing on a little problem I didn't need. Deep down I knew it was better to get rid of it than keep it; out of sight, out of mind. After that brief exchange, I simply thought no more of it and jumped in the pool. Problem solved.

Not really. The problem escalated. What I didn't realise was that Mrs Jenkins had discovered her wedding ring was missing and the news of it went up and down our street like wildfire. All the neighbours knew. I do remember her standing at our front door the next day, asking my parents if I knew anything about the missing ring. As it was no longer part of my life when they questioned me, it was effortless just to reply 'No' and continue brushing my doll's hair as if the grown-ups were nothing more than background noise. I had learnt the art of dishonesty from two older brothers who lied constantly to get someone else – namely me – into trouble. So I thought simply passing the smoking gun on to Sarah was a good plan.

What my seven-year-old brain wasn't capable of, however, was thinking a little further ahead about the impact of my actions. What I hadn't planned for was Sarah visiting her grandma – Mrs Richards, our neighbour – a week later. I also didn't have the ability to foresee that Sarah would be proudly displaying the new sparkler adorning her finger, or that she would tell her grandma she received it from a nearby resident: the young cavalier, Brett, next door.

What follows still makes me weep whenever I think about it. It was an extremely hot Saturday afternoon, so I was wearing only my swimmers around the house. Mum and Dad had just bought the weekly groceries and I was standing on a chair in the kitchen helping them unpack it all. I always found unpacking the groceries such a pleasurable experience, like unwrapping Christmas gifts. It was exciting to see what treats and desserts Mum was planning to reward us with throughout the week.

Suddenly, a knock interrupted my pleasant afternoon. Mrs Richards swung the missing ring on her index finger proudly, wearing a smug look that said, 'Just call me Miss Marple.' She was usually a pleasant lady, but on this day, she was not my favourite neighbour. After all, she could have returned the ring quietly to Mrs Jenkins and said she'd found it in the garden – problem solved. But no. I always wondered why she thought it was a good idea to tell my parents, knowing too well they were not light on dishing out punishment. There must have been an element of sadism in her.

It only took a few seconds for Mum and Dad to hear how 'Miss Marple' had solved the crime and that I was the felon. It also only took a few seconds for Dad to whisk me off the chair and throw me outside, and to search the yard for an object to punish me with. He ripped a paling off the back fence and broke it in half. I was already trembling and bawling my eyes out, begging for forgiveness. Dad swooped me up with one arm and began slapping my arse with the unshaven piece of timber. The only thing between that and my buttocks was a pair of very thin swimmers. I screamed the neighbourhood down. The pain was excruciating. I sure hope Mrs Richards heard it and felt guilty, although I doubt it. I don't know what was more traumatic: the pain inflicted on my backside, or Dad screaming down my ear.

'You little shit! This will teach you never to lie again!'

Really? Really, Dad? It did not teach me to never lie again; on the contrary, it taught me how to be a smarter liar, especially to him. This barbaric act also taught me to never trust or love him again. If only this kind of child abuse had been illegal in those days, he might have faced some consequence for his brutal actions. Unfortunately, it wasn't – especially in my backyard.

I cannot remember how long Dad kept hitting me. Time seems to stand still when your life is under threat. He only stopped the plank torture when I could gather enough breath between the screams to shout, 'Please, I want to pee!' He eventually dropped me to the ground and bellowed, 'Get inside to your bedroom and don't come out until you're told.' I was in so much pain I couldn't even feel my legs. I slowly stood up and limped inside the house, crying my eyes out. I went straight to my bedroom and immediately pulled off my swimmers to inspect the damage in the wardrobe mirror. My buttocks were red, raw and bleeding. They felt like they were on fire.

Exhausted, the life belted out of me, I collapsed face down on the bed and slept it off. Perhaps I would wake up and discover it was a horrendous nightmare. It wasn't. I woke up in the middle of the night, hungry, and realised I was actually living the nightmare. I also realised my parents hadn't even called me for dinner. Most kids wish for a new toy for Christmas; I was begging Santa for a new family and a new set of buttocks.

Part IX

Behind Closed Doors

1. Who's the Boss?

Shouting, beltings and bullying were so common in my childhood that a day without them seemed odd. My basic instincts as a child told me the maltreatment and abuse weren't normal behaviour, even though they were happening all around me: from the nuns at school to home, as well as in many families in my neighbourhood. What hope did we kids have of stopping the beltings at home when the nuns and teachers at school also released their frustrations by whacking and caning us? Was the teaching profession in those days really that stressful? Or were they agitated from excessive caffeine use? I still can't comprehend how teachers got away with corporal punishment, or how parents could physically abuse their kids and each other without any consequences.

My earliest memory of domestic abuse is the sight and sound of Dad holding Mum down on the sofa with his knee while slapping her pretty face.

'Get off me, Kevin, you friggin' bastard!'

'Don't call me a bastard, you bitch!'

'Stop it! You're hurting me!'

As Dad slapped her across the face, he yelled, 'Stop bossing me around! I'm the boss here, and you better remember it!'

It must have been really late at night; the commotion had woken the four of us boys in our bedrooms down the hallway. We all leapt up and ran down the passage, then huddled together in our pyjamas at the hallway door to see what all the noise was about. We were scared and we felt helpless. It was like watching a burning truck run through the middle of town; we couldn't do anything. We knew if we interfered to try and save Mum's pretty face, we would wake up the next morning just as bruised as her and would be lining up for her bottle of foundation. Mum had soon learnt that a yellow-tinted concealer neutralised the blue in a bruise; apply it thickly enough and the evidence almost disappears. What a shame that smearing concealer on Dad didn't make him disappear as well.

I never had much respect for authority after witnessing that.

Sunday mornings in our household were a regular shitshow. There was no chance of sleeping in. We would often wake up to Mum and Dad arguing in the bedroom. It could be over anything, such as snoring all night, the room stinking of booze or mum not getting enough attention from Dad the night before at one of the clubs in town. Mum would be jealous of Dad dancing with her best friend, Dotti, and not her. Without fail, these arguments would escalate and continue to the kitchen, complete with the clanging of plates and dishes, and the slamming of cupboards. Dad would raise his voice and mum would retaliate even louder. Eventually, the arguments would end up in a row over money. Basically, Mum was spending money faster than Dad could make it. She never was good with budgeting the fortnightly allowance Dad gave her after he'd taken out his own 'drink allowance'.

If Mum liked something, she simply bought it. If she didn't have the cash, she would simply 'lay-by' it. This was a very popular concept in Australia: you paid a deposit to secure a purchase, then you had to make regular payments until it was paid off. The drawback was that if you didn't pay it off in time, you lost the article and all the payments as well. Mum was the lay-by queen. While she nourished her wardrobe, the house and our lives using this system, she also nourished Dad's anger. His wallet was always empty, apart from the moths.

Another one of Mum's talents was being a reasonably

good cook. Like most women in the sixties, she spent a lot of time in the kitchen, baking and preparing meals. I knew this because I was often there too, helping her make scones and cakes while my three brothers were outside helping Dad mow the lawn or playing mechanics under the car bonnet. Most meals – the standard meat and three vegetables – were OK. But there were nights when Mum thought she was Julia Child and would experiment with dishes that were so disastrous, we kids would have to force ourselves to eat out of hunger. One evening, she served up a French dish called: 'Coq au vin' which is a fancy chicken in wine stew. Apparently to mum, that translated to 'rabbit in tomato sauce', because that's what she used and that's exactly what it tasted like. We forced it down, figuring it would either digest (eventually) or strengthen our immune systems. What doesn't kill you makes you stronger.

Dad wasn't quite so keen to risk missing work the next day with an upset stomach. So, after one bite, he slammed his knife and fork down on the table, jumped up, threw his Coq au vin in the garbage can, grabbed a bottle of beer and went to watch the news in the living room. I thought his behaviour was an insult to Mum's efforts. While I admit that if the dog had been allowed inside, I would have fed it to her (she loved rabbit meat), I would never have thrown it in the garbage. It was on the tip of my tongue to yell, 'You know there are starving kids in the world who would eat that?' but something instinctively told me that wouldn't be a good idea.

I could never understand how or why Mum put up with all this physical and emotional abuse. It mustn't have been easy for her with all that testosterone in the house. A husband who always drank and never gave her a compliment or any affection, together with four demanding boys and endless heat and flies, must have had her on the brink of insanity. How do you not snap and strike back at some point? Well, actually, she did.

2. A Christmas Tale

It was Christmas time, extremely hot, and the house was full of the usual Adelaide relatives on their pilgrimage to the Silver City: Mum's brother Arthur, his wife Madge and their family, together with my grandparents, who we affectionately called Nanna and Pa. They must all have been closeted masochists to endure that tedious six-hour drive to the desert in the scorching heat, only to spend three or four painful weeks living with my family in our three-bedroom, one-toilet home. The place was so full and so hot that most nights all the kids would end up grabbing a pillow and a sheet and sleeping on the lawn. The house was an oven and Mum and Dad's heated arguments only added to the temperature.

It was nothing out of the ordinary for us kids to nod off to sleep each night to the lullaby of Mum and Dad shouting at each other – and it didn't matter who else was around. Dad would come home drunk from the pub each evening, have a few more beers and really get under Mum's skin. They would lie in bed shouting, with Mum threatening to annihilate Dad the moment he went to sleep. Mind you, she didn't really mind it when Dad had drunk himself into unconsciousness; it was a great opportunity to raid his wallet. And the next morning, when he ranted and raved that his money was gone, she always managed to convince him he'd spent it all on grog.

Anyhow, this particular Christmas holiday, Dad was drunk as a skunk, and all the family were being lulled to sleep by the two of them quarrelling. Mum was at the end of her tether and the heat was getting to her. I think she may have heard that day that a couple of Christmas lay-bys she hadn't paid off in time were being placed back on the shelf, so she was pissed off, big time. She grabbed a butcher's knife from the kitchen drawer, placed it under her pillow and shouted, 'I'm warning you, Kevin. I'm sick of your drinking! When you go to sleep, I'm going to fucking stab you.' I don't understand why she never let Dad just collapse on the bed in a drunken stupor; she would egg him on and make him go from happy drunk to provoked drunk. I'm not sure what she hoped to gain from it. Maybe she'd had enough of going to bed with a drunk.

That evening, Dad had had enough of Mum as well. We all heard him shout, 'Shut up!', and we all heard the loud slap that followed. Then there was a lull. Although we were shocked by the slap, we were all relieved it was over; finally there would be some peace and we could go to sleep. My brother and I had put a thick blanket on the hard linoleum floor of our room and, because it was so hot, only a sheet to cover us to keep the mosquitoes from biting. We were in between the single beds where my Uncle Arthur and Aunty Madge slept.

As we settled down, enjoying the new peace, Dad's sudden scream broke the silence. 'Aargh! The bitch stabbed me! The bloody bitch stabbed me!'

Wow. Maybe there is a God. I sat up and turned to Trevor with a huge smile on my face. 'Oh my God! Mum stabbed Dad!'

Dad continued going berserk, shouting the house down. He must have been delirious. He was drunk, angry, confused and tired, and he had just been stabbed by his own wife.

Mum, realising she had gone a little bit too far, panicked and ran into our bedroom in her two-piece pink pyjamas, still holding the knife. She came right up to my face in the dark, her hair in curlers with a bright yellow scarf around it, and said, 'Brett, quick! Lock me in the wardrobe and don't tell your father where I am!' The things I had to do. I scrambled up, pushed her into my wardrobe, locked it and jumped back into my makeshift bed as fast as I could. I lay there like nothing had happened, my aunty and uncle silently feigning sleep on either side of me. Dad was still yelping like a wounded dog, and I was beginning to get worried; not about him, but about how long Mum could breathe in a wardrobe full of clothes, smelly shoes, scraps of material and dolls. It must have been really uncomfortable in there.

I noticed no one was rushing out of bed to help Dad, which said a lot. He staggered from his bedroom and began sniffing through the house like a police dog, trying to hunt her down. He went to my older brothers' room first, turned on the light and shouted, 'Where's your mother? The bitch stabbed me!' Mick and David were also sleeping on the floor in makeshift beds, between my Nanna and Pa who had commandeered my brothers' single beds. I heard my Nanna's distinct high-pitched croaky voice. 'She's not here. She's probably in the kitchen sharpening the knife. Now piss off and let me sleep.' That old girl was tough as nails and had a great sense of humour. I loved her. She never really had time for Dad; I think she always resented him getting her only daughter pregnant and taking her away from the city to no man's land. The wedding photos show everyone smiling except for Nanna, who looks bitter and unimpressed.

Dad came to our bedroom next, turned on the light and shouted, 'Where's the bitch? Is she in here?' We all raised our heads and acted as if we had no idea what he was talking about. He stood there in his pyjama shorts and no top, holding the wound on his giant beer belly. There was blood all over his hands and shorts, but it wasn't spurting out; Mum must have only lacerated him with a short, shallow cut. There was more blood in Dad's face from fury. We all mumbled 'No' and hoped he would wander off before he spotted Trevor staring at the wardrobe.

He did.

My uncle jumped out of bed and started to get dressed. I think he'd had enough of seeing his big sister being victimised all these years by his brutal brother-in-law; the time had come, he thought, to get the law involved. He ran outside to the neighbours – they had a telephone – and stood at their fence shouting, 'Call the boys in blue! Call the boys in blue!' (I'm not sure why he couldn't just say 'police'.)

The neighbours, who were very conservative and didn't want to bring attention to the neighbourhood, came running out in their nightwear, wondering what all the commotion was about. They saw my dad stumbling around on the verandah and soon realised he wasn't going to die from the wound. 'No point getting the police involved, Arthur. Just bandage the wound and put Kevin back to bed. Everything will be all right in the morning.'

The attitude towards domestic violence in the 1960s was so different to today's. It was considered a private family matter. The neighbours wanted to keep it that way, so my aunty and uncle cleaned Dad up and put him to bed to sleep it off. As he lost his hold on consciousness, I was busy helping Mum regain hers by releasing her from the wardrobe. When the pandemonium was over, everyone including Mum crawled back into bed and went back to sleep.

I woke up the next morning to the sound of the kettle whistling. I was expecting all the relatives to have packed their suitcases and abandoned ship, and Mum and Dad to be arguing and spilling blood again. I was not expecting to find everyone in the kitchen having breakfast and playing happy families. It was as if nothing at all had happened. The ladies of this civilised household were busy cooking eggs and toast, nibbling as they served the men and kids gathered around the table. Nanna was at the front of the house in her nightie with a head full of curlers and clips, watering the few flowers in the garden rather than helping in the kitchen. Perhaps she thought too many cooks would spoil the broth, or perhaps she felt as baffled and surprised as me.

I went out to greet her. 'Nanna, did Mum stab Dad last night?'

Still staring at the garden, she replied quickly, 'Yes, dear,' as if I'd just asked her a trivial question. It was clear from her response and body language that there was nothing else to be said. Life goes on. I stood with her for a moment, gazing at the plants, before she broke the silence. 'Run along now and get some breakfast, dear.'

I toddled off inside and joined the actors at the breakfast table.

Part X

Pets

1. Zoophobia

Some people love pets, and some people don't. I get it.

My dad had zoophobia: a fear of animals. Actually, he didn't really have a fear; he simply didn't like them. But then he didn't seem to like humans much, either. I think his hatred of pets might have had a lot to do with his upbringing: his parents were working-class people, times were tough, and they found it enough of a struggle to feed and take care of their kids, let alone a pet.

I always wondered if Dad had suffered a trauma as a child – maybe he'd been bitten by a dog or a cat sat on his face during his sleep – as he really had no time for animals at all. The moment a neighbourhood dog or cat wandered accidentally into our yard, he would spring up from his chair like a rocket, roll up his newspaper as a weapon and run out to the yard, shouting and hissing. 'Gone! Pssss! Piss off, you mongrel!' Dad didn't want the creature marking its territory in our yard, but it would end up shitting itself from shock anyway. If Dad noticed a neighbour sitting on their verandah watching him abuse their beloved pet, he would often shut down immediately from guilt and wander back inside with *his* tail between his legs. You can traumatise your own family all you like, but you have to keep the neighbours happy.

Dad was a practical man; pets seemed useless to him, a waste of time and money. However, he probably wouldn't have barked at someone giving him a goat or a kangaroo. He would have attached it to the fence with a long chain so it could eat the grass and save him mowing the lawns on Sunday mornings. He wouldn't say no to a cow either, if it would give milk daily, and if its luck ran out, he would dispose of it on the barbecue. Dad thought animals were dirty and he couldn't grasp how people would let them inside the house. He reckoned pets only caused havoc, mayhem and disease.

We let Dad in the house, though.

Pets require a lot of love and affection, but when they get it, they give a lot back. I actually think the real issue with Dad hating pets was that affection was an alien concept to him. Pets would have made him too vulnerable. If he was seen to be caring and lovey-dovey towards them, the family would be lining up behind them expecting their share as well.

As for me, I love animals and loved having pets. The only ones I got were left to me by people who had died, and Dad couldn't refuse them. But, thanks to the deceased, the few pets I had brought brief joy into my life. They were a source of the unconditional love that didn't otherwise exist in my household. However, I never really had much luck with them. I did my best with each and every one – but I know that when I die, I am going to Pet Hell.

2. Chatterbox

Mum, my brothers and I were settled in the living room one evening watching television when we got the shock of our lives. There wasn't a power cut, nor was our favourite show cancelled. No, Dad walked in, holding a birdcage with a budgerigar in it. We knew how much he hated pets, so we thought he must have won second prize in a raffle. He stood there, staring at the cage, and declared, 'Digit died and left me this bloody budgie.'

Digit was one of his many drinking mates from the pub. His real name was Frank, but because he'd lost a couple of fingers in a mining accident, his friends gave him the new nickname. Getting a nickname is a very common thing in Australia, and when your friends honour you with one, you don't have a choice; you have to accept it. I knew a guy at school who was super thin, so he scored the nickname 'Skin', for 'skinny'. My mother's name is Shirley, but Dad only called her 'Girl' and hardly ever said her real name. Either it was because she always looked so young and pretty, or he was playing it safe to avoid slipping up and calling her by a different woman's name when he was drunk. And I've already told you that according to my brothers, my nickname was Betty. If only I had lost a couple of fingers.

Even though Dad hated pets, he felt obligated to keep the budgie out of respect for Digit. That is what best mates do in Australia. You're friends for life and you stick by each other. But he couldn't be bothered taking care of it, so he staggered towards me, plonked the cage by my side and said, 'Here, take care of it. His name's Chatterbox'. I think somewhere in the back of Dad's inebriated mind he thought the bird stood a better chance of survival with me than if he gave it to my brothers. In any case, they looked very relieved the responsibility hadn't been given to them.

I was only eight years old. Any gift from Dad was considered a bonus; he could have handed me a brick and I would have jumped for joy. But Chatterbox came in a cage with all the trimmings: water container, food bowl, some tiny toys and a little mirror to convince him he had a friend. I accepted the gift with pleasure and couldn't wait to shower it with love; I was dizzy with the hope of getting something positive in return. I placed the birdcage centre stage in the kitchen for everyone to see, hoping Chatterbox would bring some joy and peace to the family.

Chatterbox was a cute thing, with green wings and a yellow head and tummy. I wanted to rename him Pretty Boy, but Dad wasn't having it. He told me I had to stick with Chatterbox out of respect for Digit. Right. He didn't seem to have any respect for the bird, apart from the fact it wore the national colours of Australia.

It only took one night for the family to start hating Chatterbox's guts and wishing the tiny creature a horrible death. Even though the cage was covered at night with a large tea towel (apparently to help it sleep and prevent night frights), the budgie was clearly an insomniac. It didn't shut up all night. You might think the sweet singing of a bird would help you drift gently off to sleep, but no: Chatterbox's chirp was a high-pitched garble that made you slowly go insane. I'm not sure why Digit named it Chatterbox. Earbasher would have been more appropriate.

Next morning, I woke up with a start. Dad was standing beside my bed, holding the cage. Chatterbox was swinging and hissing at an unbelievable volume. Dad, a man of few words, hissed just as loudly, 'Shut the budgie up, or I'm going to break its neck,' and dropped the cage on my bed like a hot brick.

I wasn't sure what he was expecting me to do. Tape its beak every night? Put it under my pillow? If Digit hadn't expired, Dad would have returned Chatterbox in a flash.

I moved Chatterbox swiftly from centre stage in the kitchen to stage left in the laundry, where the bird definitely got a lot quieter. Mum reckoned it was depressed from the isolation; budgies are social beings. I think it was traumatised and had probably completely lost its hearing thanks to the ear-splitting washing machine. When that thing hit the spin cycle, you would have sworn there was a helicopter in the laundry. It was never levelled on the floor and all the tub bearings had worn out.

Apparently, you're supposed to clean a budgie's cage thoroughly once a week. Nobody told me. After a few months had passed, the cage stank from all the bird droppings and the laundry was covered with feathers and debris. Mum couldn't face doing the washing any more. It was a sign for me to give Chatterbox's home a spring clean. So one sunny day, I grabbed some rags and a bucket of soapy water and took the cage to the backyard. It would be a ritual washing, a bonding moment between me and my lovely sweet Chatterbox. I slid the bottom tray out and cleaned it. Chatterbox was chirping with joy at the thought of finally having a clean toilet. After I opened the cage door to grab the mirror and toys, Chatterbox jumped around all over the place to avoid being whacked by my arm. He was springing around the cage so much that he burst out through the cage door before I could stop him.

I couldn't believe it. He hopped about on the lawn, turned around and stared at me. The look on his face said, 'What the hell am I hopping for? I can fly!' I stared back at him, gently whispering, 'No, Chatterbox. Please. No. Come here.' Tears welled up in my eyes. As I stretched my arms out to beckon him, Chatterbox stretched his wings out, waving goodbye. He saw his opportunity and grabbed it. He flapped those little wings and soared high into the sky.

After watching Chatterbox disappear into his new world, I sat gazing at the empty cage, tears rolling gently down my face. I had mixed feelings. I was sad to have lost love and a good friend. I was stunned at how swiftly and simply Chatterbox had escaped from his hell hole. More than anything, I was angry he didn't take me with him.

3. Fishy Business

We always had lovely neighbours. When I was about nine years old, on one side we had the O'Briens – a lovely couple called John and Lila, with their two teenage boys, Barry and Gregory – and on the other side we had an elderly couple, Harriet and Nelson Richards. They were the odd ones out in our street. They were the only ones who were refined; they always looked after their house and their beautiful rose garden. Mum used to make scones every Sunday morning, and I was always chosen to be the delivery boy and take a plateful to Harriet and Nelson. I never minded doing it; Harriet would always invite me in for a few minutes to look at her massive aquarium, which was a prominent feature in their living room. I say *her* aquarium, because it was Harriet's baby, her pet project and her responsibility to feed the fish and clean the tank. That tank was spectacular. It must have been over one and a half metres wide; it had plants, little bridges and tiny temples, and was full of the most colourful fish I had ever seen. It had so many gadgets whirling, spinning and blowing bubbles. I was always mesmerised. To a little boy like me, it was Atlantis – a whole new world underwater.

Unfortunately, the weekly delivery of scones came to a sudden halt when Harriet died in her sleep one night. This left Nelson devastated and forced him to think about his future. He wasn't certain what he was going to do – stay or leave. However, one thing he did know: he certainly wasn't going to be feeding the fish and cleaning the tank. He was more concerned with how he was going to feed himself. Since I was a regular visitor who showed an interest in the fish and Mum was a very dear friend of Harriet's, Nelson convinced Mum to take the huge fish tank. Needless to say, Dad was not impressed, but Mum swiftly reminded him, 'Well, we did it for Digit, so now we do it for Harriet.'

The aquarium was moved carefully into our living room and placed under a window next to the television, which was really handy; every time the boring ads came on, we would turn our attention to the fish tank and be entertained by bubbles instead. Sometimes Trevor and I would stand in front of the aquarium for hours with our noses glued to the glass, watching the fish swimming around aimlessly. We would often tap the glass to get their attention, but they just ignored us. They must have been deaf. We always wondered if the fish saw our huge faces against the glass and thought we were sea monsters. Sometimes we would entertain ourselves by naming them all. I would give them lovely names like Sunshine, Flipper or Wings; Trevor was less kind (albeit cute) and called them Sardines, Poopsie or Pork Chops. Now and then my older brothers – who had inherited Dad's dislike for pets – would insult these beautiful creatures, calling them Slimeface, Conehead or Puss.

My job was to feed the fish and clean the tank. Feeding was fun, but cleaning it was tough and tedious. They say you're supposed to remove the fish and water first, but I could never be bothered. I would submerge my little arms and face to scrub the glass and wipe the ornaments, and I would end up wetter than the fish. It was too big a job for a kid. While the tank did have a filter system, it never worked very well. I could never get the glass clean – it was continually covered with slime – and I would always see more floating fish poop than fish.

My hometown, being in the middle of the desert, had water restrictions and what little water we had was full of fluoride and chlorine to kill bacteria. As part of the maintenance routine, I was supposed to measure the pH levels in the tank to keep the fish happy, but I had no idea what I was doing. The tank started to smell like a swimming pool. The chlorine in their water must have almost blinded the fish, as they would often crash into each other. When I thought about it, I realised the water in the local swimming pool always stung my eyes and left them bloodshot – and the fish had to live in this same water. There was no hope for them. They started losing their colour from the bleach . . . and eventually each one in turn acquired its final name: Floater.

Dad refused to replace the fish; he said it was costing too much in electricity and water. So, after each fish blew its last bubble, Dad would either throw it to the neighbour's cat or send it on a journey down the toilet. Harriet would have turned in her grave if she'd seen the state of her beloved fish tank. Before we knew it, the tank was in drought and sent on a journey to the back shed. It took a few months before Dad convinced one of his drinking mates to take it off his hands.

So I failed at caring for flying animals and didn't have much more success looking after the swimming ones. There was only one thing left: a mammal called Sandy.

4. Sandy

Nelson, now a widower, bought a young Labrador dog as a companion to fill the void from losing his wife. The dog was named Sandy, for her lovely golden sand colour. She was the cutest thing. When Nelson got lucky and met another lady companion, it wasn't long before they decided to leave town and start a new life together. His new girlfriend wasn't keen on taking Sandy, and since Nelson had dumped the fish on us, he thought he could dump the dog in the same place. Dad only saw a ball of debt being handed over to us, but he reluctantly accepted Sandy because Nelson worked on the mines – as usual, mates helped each other out. We collected Sandy on the day we bade farewell to Nelson and his new love.

Dad swiftly made his point that we kids were to take care of the dog and that he wouldn't be buying any food for it. It was to stay outside and be fed only scraps from dinner, eating what we ate. If the RSPCA had existed then, I would have reported him for animal abuse and asked them to collect Sandy, and with a bit of luck, me as well.

As usual, my brothers didn't have a caring bone in their bodies and totally left the responsibility for Sandy to me. I was fine with that; I had something to love and care for once again. The only problem was, I had no idea how to raise a dog properly. I couldn't even save a fish, let alone a dog. I'd have to give Sandy a 'Dog of the Century' award, just for her patience, loyalty and basic tolerance of our family. She got unlucky, though. They say you can only kick a dog so many times before it walks away, but Sandy never took her chances. The gate was always open, but she never escaped. Silly dog.

Dad couldn't be bothered building a kennel for her, so like a wild animal, Sandy had to face the weather and seasons all year, from extreme heat to freezing nights. She would move strategically around the yard to find any kind of shelter from the scorching sun, wicked dust storms, or frosty nights. She learnt to eat whatever was left over from our dinner – anything from fish fingers to the infamous Coq au vin. She also developed a taste for Chinese takeout, Kentucky Fried Chicken bones and pizza crusts.

One Saturday afternoon when everyone was at the

football, I stayed home because the weather was freezing, stormy, wet and miserable. I hated football enough without having to endure ghastly weather for the privilege. I looked outside and saw Sandy soaked and trembling with cold. It was time for her to have a treat, or at least a bit of mercy. I grabbed some towels, placed them in front of the gas heater in the living room and called her inside. I laid her on the towels, wiped her down and patted her to sleep. She must have been dreaming she was in dog heaven. She also must have been thinking, 'Ahhh, about bloody time.' I lay beside her, warm, cosy and peaceful . . .

Unfortunately, I dozed off.

Unfortunately, the family came home from football.

They walked into the house and saw the two of us snoozing away in front of the heater. Sandy and I both woke from fright at the screaming. Dad was shouting, 'Get that bloody dog outside!' and Mum was shouting, 'Get that bloody dog off my towels!' My brothers always rejoiced when I got in trouble, so they added fuel to the fire. 'Oh my God!' 'I can't believe you did that!' 'You've got to be joking!' I hated them so much.

Dad kicked Sandy outside, and Mum hurled the towels into the washing machine. I was given a whack by Dad and thrown into my bedroom, missing dinner altogether. For what? Yes, for caring.

Years passed, and Sandy watched me grow into a teenager. I watched her gain a lot of weight and her back legs deteriorating; eventually she dragged them along whenever she moved. She was also incredibly overweight. Poor thing. I thought Sandy and I had a lot in common when it came to neglect. We just smiled and put up with all the crap. We couldn't run away, for we had nowhere to go, and neither of us had any idea whether the grass was greener on the other side. Better the devil you know. We both soldiered on.

One quiet Sunday afternoon, we had finished the traditional roast dinner and Mum had gone to see a lady about getting new curtains made for the living room. I had just fed Sandy with the leftovers from lunch and told Mum I'd wash all the dishes so she could get to the curtain lady on time. I stood at the sink, which had a huge wide window above it that looked out to the backyard. While washing a dish, I would look out to the ugly, dusty backyard with its rusted shed and poor excuse for a lawn. There was a fence that had lost so many palings over time it looked like my Grandpa Jack's teeth. The fence was no good for keeping anything in or out. I would often daydream about making the backyard look inviting – a large covered patio, garden furniture, new iron fence, lots of trees along the back, a decent barbecue . . . All of a sudden, I saw David and Dad pulling Sandy by the collar to the small patch of lawn. *How sweet*, I thought. *They're finally going to give Sandy a much-needed wash.* But I didn't see any hose or soap.

What I did see, however, was David raising a BB gun and Dad holding Sandy down with his foot. I couldn't believe my eyes. David started shooting at Sandy's head as I yelled 'Noooooo! Sandy!' from the kitchen. I felt like I was watching a horror movie on the big screen.

I threw my rubber gloves off into the sink and ran outside to the backyard. I knelt and hugged Sandy, shouting, 'Why?'

My brother said, 'Get off her or I will shoot you next.'

Dad butted in. 'She's too old. She's clogged up and can't walk anymore.'

I looked up. 'Well, Grandma's the same. Are you going to shoot her, too?'

David ignored my pleas, pushed me aside and continued shooting slugs into Sandy's head until she stopped moving completely. Dad dragged her to the back fence, through a couple of missing palings and into a hole they had dug in the regeneration area earlier that morning. Sandy died that day; a little part of me did too. I asked Mum years later why Dad hadn't called the vet to put her to sleep. She replied, 'Too expensive, love. Much cheaper with a gun and just bury her out the back.'

It was all about the money. You better watch out, Grandma.

Part XI

Being Catholic

1. Catholic Primary School

My hometown, Broken Hill, always had a huge Catholic community – so large that each suburb (there were four) had its own elementary school and church. The Catholic high school and cathedral were in the centre of town, perched on a high hill – prime real estate, of course. I spent eleven years in Catholic education, and although I considered myself a good Catholic boy, I'd have to admit my mum and dad probably deserved a refund based on my 'impure thoughts' alone.

It was a typical Catholic school: weekly confessions and masses, meatless Fridays during Lent, and special events such as First Holy Communion and Confirmation. It had its own Bible, called the catechism, and we would learn about extraordinary things like purgatory, a place where you would go when you died if you had some unresolved leftover sins. Christians back home on earth would have to pray or pay the Church to try to get you a ticket to heaven. Then there was limbo – a place between heaven and hell where babies who didn't get the chance to be baptised Catholic would end up. Really?

My elementary school was called All Saints Primary School. *All* Saints? Not one, but all of them? Either someone couldn't be bothered choosing a particular holy person's name for the school, or they were way too ambitious. Most of the teachers were Sisters of Mercy and Marist Brothers, but there were also a few non-clergy people who added a bit of colour to the staff wardrobe.

The playground only had asphalt – no grass – so you can imagine how busy the teachers were nursing and bandaging grazed hands and knees. Summer was a killer, playing outside with no trees for cooling off. They would give us free cartons of flavoured milk for comfort and joy. These had usually sat in crates in the hot sun all morning, so the teachers were often wiping up vomit from the rancid milk.

The school was a brick and steel building, two stories high, with a canteen (or 'tuck shop' as we call it in Australia) in the basement. Here lunches, sweets and soft drinks were sold. The parents would volunteer and be rostered to man the tuck shop during lunch and recesses. I loved it when it was Mum's turn; she would give me free sweets. I knew it wasn't right, but would happily use them to bribe people to play with me or be my friend that day. Despite that, I still told Mum she would go to hell for handing out treats for free. She said she wasn't baptised Catholic, so she was safe. That sounded good to me.

All Saints Primary School was tolerable . . . but the punishments those nuns and brothers executed were insufferable. Virtually anything could set them off and bring down the wrath of the clergy: wisecracking, talking and fooling around in church, failing to do your homework, teasing someone, questioning any of the Catholic practices, being happy, or even just breathing. We would do anything to keep on the right side of the staff, whether it was a small gift of chocolates or some flowers from the garden, a compliment, or an over-the-top greeting like, 'Good morning, Sister Frances Xavier Cabrini of the Annunciation, may God bless you.'

I tried to impress them one day with a story about my grandpa, who had told me he was born in Jerusalem. I couldn't believe my ears. I couldn't wait to tell the nuns at school that my Pa was born in the same Holy Land as Jesus – especially in Jerusalem, the city where Jesus had preached in the temples and performed his healing miracles. This news of my Pa being born in one of the world's oldest religious cities and the thought that Jesus, too, had wandered around there made me feel really special. I felt I even had closer connections to Jesus than the nuns did. Perhaps my Pa's parents had even visited one of the temples where Jesus delivered his sermons centuries before. I never doubted my Pa came from Israel, because of his olive skin and dark hair.

The nuns were impressed with my news and I was their golden student for a few weeks. But I was keen to get even more brownie points from the teachers; I needed to extract some more details about my Pa's extraordinary connections to the Holy Land.

Mum was ironing in the living room, watching the telly.

'Mum, how old was Pa when he came to Australia?'

'What? What are you talking about?' Only half-listening to me, she continued ironing her frock.

'Pa – he was born in Jerusalem. How old was he when he left there to come to Australia?'

'What do you mean? He was born here.'

'But he told me he was born in Jerusalem.'

'Yes. Jerusalem is a little town in South Australia, a couple of hours north of Adelaide.'

Mum's eyes were still glued to the screen; I put myself in between her and the television so I had her full attention.

'What? Really? There's a Jerusalem in South Australia?'

'Yes, why? Now move away from the telly. I'm watching this.'

I persisted.

'But, Mum . . . you're sure it's that one where Pa came from, and not the one where Jesus lived?'

Mum slammed the iron down on the ironing board.

'Yes, Brett. He was born here. He's never left the country. Now don't be bloody stupid. Move.'

Embarrassment began to creep up my neck. 'Oh no.' I whispered to myself.

'What? What have you done now?' asked mum.

'Umm . . . nothing.'

I swiftly left the room.

Surely I could never go back to school and face those nuns again. I felt like I had committed the greatest sin of all time. I couldn't tell anyone at school that I'd made a mistake, that Pa wasn't really born in the same country as Jesus. I couldn't bear to mention it at confession with the priest, and I avoided mentioning the topic ever again at school. It was a complete secret, between me and Jesus.

Had they known I got the Jerusalem thing totally wrong, the wrath of the nuns would have been unbearable. The nuns at school were very unpredictable; you would never know how they might react. But I learnt very quickly to read their mood, stay away and practise looking like a statue. Acting like a regular eight-year-old kid around a grumpy, frustrated nun wasn't worth the pain and torture.

Actually, we had to be equally careful around the lay teachers. I had a teacher in Grade 3 called Mrs Spiteri. She had very dark curly hair, a long, protruding nose and bulging eyes. It was the 1960s and she loved wearing miniskirts – very short ones. It must have made the nuns cringe or feel jealous. I liked Mrs Spiteri, but she was a wolf in sheep's clothing. You had to stay on the right side of her or she would make your life miserable – just like a nun, really.

One of the boys who sat next to me in this grade was Bernard Cooper. He had an eating disorder called pica: an appetite for eating things that are not considered food. I believe kids often put non-food items in their mouths because they're curious about the world around them, but I think Bernard did it because he had a massive tapeworm in his gut; he always had hunger pangs, was irritable and was constantly scratching his bum. It's quite common in Australia to give kids deworming tablets every year, as threadworm and tapeworm are common. Schools send reminder newsletters about it to parents. I don't think Bernard's mum, Mrs Cooper, ever received one of those newsletters; Bernard probably ate them. Sitting next to him was often risky. You never knew what he was going to eat next. I watched him chomp away half of his school tie, one sleeve of his jumper, a small notebook and most of his shirt collar. Even though I tried really hard to keep my belongings close to me, Bernard also managed over time to eat half my wooden ruler, a few coloured pencils and my coloured eraser collection. I was so angry I told the teacher and asked if I could move to another seat.

Mrs Spiteri was not impressed with him.

'Bernard Cooper, stand up!'

'Why?'

'Because I said so.'

Bernard gave a heavy sigh, dragged himself to his feet and leaned against the corner of the desk behind him, hands in his pockets. He couldn't have cared less about being in trouble.

He shrugged. 'What did I do?'

'What did you do? You ate all of Brett's things! Take a look at yourself – you've even eaten half your clothes! What's wrong with you?'

Bernard didn't care what people thought, and he wasn't at all bothered by Mrs Spiteri. But his tapeworm obviously thought differently. It must have suddenly woken up and irritated him. Bernard snapped. 'I don't know! What's wrong with *you*, Miss?'

Mrs Spiteri was furious. She marched to the classroom door and flung it open.

'Bernard Cooper, leave the classroom right now and go sit outside the principal's office!'

The whole class stopped working and put their pencils down to watch the drama. Bernard slouched towards the door and stopped directly in front of Mrs Spiteri, who was blocking the door with her arm.

Red-faced, she glared at him and yelled, 'Bernard Cooper! Don't you know it's rude to walk in front of someone? Get behind me!'

Bernard raised his chin. 'My dad told me never to walk

behind horses.'

Mrs Spiteri grabbed what was left of his collar and dragged him to the principal's office. Once they had exited the classroom, the rest of us burst out laughing.

We never saw Bernard again after that day and were never sure what happened to him. But we knew he would be OK; however bad the situation got, he could always eat himself out of it.

It was always wise, if you could, to act tough and never show your weakness to authority. You were more of a target to the teachers if you cried, screamed or ran out of the classroom when they smacked you. They didn't care what they used to punish you with. It was mostly their hands, the cane, or a ruler across your knuckles or buttocks, but they would also grab whatever else was close to hand: a feather duster, a belt, a Bible. We all got better at taking punishment without flinching. I got a lot of practice at home with Dad's major whacks, so school punishment was usually a breeze . . . until one day in Grade 4, when I was about nine years old.

A group of tough boys, the 'troublemakers' from my class, were throwing stones at each other during first recess, as a game. Unfortunately, one of the stones went over the fence and chipped a car's windscreen. Even more unfortunately, the owner – who was outside gardening at the time – heard the impact and reported it to Sister Mary Kathryn, the school principal. Sister Mary Kathryn was not a happy chappy; she kept all the Grade 4 boys in, scolded us and said, 'If the boys who threw that rock don't own up by the end of lunch, all of you will be punished.'

Needless to say, at lunchtime those cool, tough lads went around to every boy in Grade 4 and threatened us. 'If you say we did it, we'll bash you up after school.'

Fear works. We kept silent, and no one owned up after lunch. What we didn't expect was the retribution from Sister Mary Kathryn the next morning. I was expecting to write out a hundred lines, pick up papers in the playground or say ten Hail Marys.

What actually happened was this: Sister Mary Kathryn lined up all the Grade 4 boys in the courtyard, an arm's distance apart. It was freezing cold, but we were all wearing shorts because it was sports day. Sister Mary Kathryn held a long cord from an old Venetian blind. She marched up and down behind us, whipping our little legs as she went. The pain was excruciating, and the cold didn't help. Some of us jumped up and down rubbing our legs, others screamed; a few peed their pants.

To me and many of my classmates, it was a sin to call these vicious women Sisters of Mercy.

2. Altar Boy

Almost every Catholic boy had a go at being an altar boy at some point during their life sentence at school. Some boys were really committed to it and did it for years. I gave it a go when I was around nine years old, mainly because I liked the idea of dressing up in something unusual and performing in front of an audience. Also, heading to Mass and being a priest's offsider was a much more peaceful way to start a Sunday morning than lying in bed listening to Mum and Dad shout and argue. Being an altar boy was voluntary – a bit of a slave's job, really. However, I figured it gave me brownie points with God, and I was always hoping the priest might give me reduced penance after confessions.

After saving up those divine brownie points, I think I lost them all in one morning when I was an altar boy with Alberto Cavelli, a kid a year older than me. Sometimes they would pair boys up for the Mass. Unfortunately, this may not have been the best pairing. Alberto always made me laugh, which wasn't a good thing during Mass. I'm not sure why he was interested in being an altar boy because he was a wild one, a real joker. He probably did it for the same reason as me: to get a break from a dysfunctional home. Part of our job was to help the priest get dressed for Mass and unrobe afterwards, and to clean up the sacristy when the service was over and everyone was gone. I can see how priests could take advantage of altar boys in this situation but, thankfully, they never looked at me. How lucky was that?

When Mass was finished, the priest told Alberto and me to clean everything up as he had to rush to do something important. This included putting the hymn books back at the end of each pew and discarding the empty vessels that held the consecrated bread and wine. We would hang up our own robes and gently fold away the priest's regalia in the large drawers in the sacristy. When everything was packed away and the church was all clear, Alberto suggested we secretly grab the key and take a look inside the tabernacle, to see Jesus. The tabernacle is a fixed, locked box in which they store the Eucharist, the communion bread which Catholics believe is the body of Christ. The tabernacle always seemed mysterious to us, as it was locked and covered with a little curtain. The priest would always stand in front of it during Mass so we couldn't see inside. But we both believed Jesus was in there – and this was our chance to say hello to Him.

We grabbed the key from the drawer in the sacristy and rushed over to the tabernacle. I was petrified, not only of being caught but also of Jesus jumping out, grabbing us and prematurely restoring us to heaven. A Catholic kid's imagination was truly wild. We stood in front of the box, teased the tiny curtains apart and placed the key in the lock.

'Are you ready?' Alberto said. 'Let's see Jesus.'

He turned the key. I held my breath.

Just as the box clicked unlocked, a huge deep voice behind us shouted, 'Boys! What are you doing?'

Oh my God. We nearly died a thousand deaths. I thought it was Jesus shouting at us. If only we'd been that lucky. Spinning around, we saw Father Rufus hovering over us with fury in his eyes and froth in the corners of his mouth. Where on earth had he suddenly come from? He was beside himself. Alberto immediately wet his pants, and I nearly shit mine. Alberto started crying hysterically, but his dismay didn't affect Father Rufus in the least. He told us we had disgraced ourselves in the eyes of God. Needless to say, our days as altar boys were numbered. Father Rufus said we couldn't be trusted anymore. Coming from a priest, how ironic is that?

3. Mum, the Heathen

Dad and the kids were all Catholics, but Mum was baptised in the Church of England or something else protestant. I was surprised Dad's family allowed him to marry a non-Catholic, but I guess since she was knocked up, they had no choice. Accidents do happen.

It was quite common on the weekends for parish priests to do the rounds, visiting families and getting free cake and coffee. I remember them visiting Mum on the odd Sunday afternoon. She would get all hysterical, cleaning the living room, baking cakes and scones, and putting out her best tea set for the holy visitors. I think they made extra trips to visit Mum because they discovered she wasn't baptised Catholic; they probably wanted to work on converting her as soon as possible, to save on all the time and prayers trying to get her out of limbo later.

One Sunday afternoon, Father Cagley and Father McCarthy came to visit Mum for afternoon tea and some light indoctrination. She sent all of us kids out to play for the entire afternoon to give her the space and freedom to drool over the delectable Father Cagley. I was only seven or eight years old. I was down at the end of the street playing with some friends when some teenage kids came by and started trying to mess up our game. They were teasing us and calling us terrible names. I knew most of the bad words they were shouting, but one of them was unfamiliar.

I'd had enough of the bullies, so I decided to abandon the games and head home, having completely forgotten about Mum entertaining the clergy. I walked straight into the living room, shouting, 'Mum! What's masturbation?'

Mum spat her tea out, but the priests seemed rather amused – fascinated, even. I could have sworn Father

McCarthy was just about to open his mouth and explain. But Mum, glaring, shoved a biscuit at me and hissed, 'Get outside. Get out and don't come back in until I tell you so.' I was like a dog: give me a treat and I would do anything. I grabbed the biscuit, smiled innocently at the priests and ran outside.

After numerous afternoon teas with Father Cagley and fearmongering from the family, Mum decided to change her religion. Dad's family convinced her that if she didn't hurry up and become Catholic, she could end up lost in limbo with all the other losers. She was given a catechism and lots of literature to plough through to understand how to be a good Catholic. I never saw her read any of it, but eventually the special day arrived: Mum's baptism. The whole family got dressed up to the nines for the occasion. Mum was wearing a very short, tight-fitting white frock and white glossy shoes, with a tiny white bow in her hair. As pure as the driven snow. She said it was important to wear white to show her 'purity of faith'. I wasn't really surprised by her choice of colour; I was more surprised she knew those words.

Mum was really buzzing that morning; she saw it as more of an outing than a serious religious conversion. She was wearing so much make-up she looked like she'd been attacked by a box of crayons. Dad wore the only suit he had – his wedding suit – and a long thin black tie, and greased his hair with Brylcreem. We all jumped into our white 1960s Ford Falcon with its red interior, and headed to All Saints Church in Piper Street. The baptism was going to be held as part of the usual Sunday morning Mass, so the church had a full congregation. With a last-minute change to the priests' rosters, Father Rufus conducted the Mass and baptism. Mum was so disappointed that she almost lost her new-found faith in the Church; she had wanted the suave, charming Father Cagley. But he was too busy out and about recruiting and flirting with other potential Catholics.

After communion, Mum and the family were invited to gather around the baptismal font. Father Rufus assumed

Mum had been studying the catechism for weeks and was knowledgeable about Catholicism; he was hoping she could recite a passage or two from memory. He tapped the microphone and asked her a standard open-ended question: 'So, Shirley, why do you want to become Catholic?'

Dad's family, being committed Catholics, were expecting Mum to say something so profound that even the Pope would have sat up and listened. Instead, she grabbed the microphone and said without any hesitation, 'I want to become Catholic so when I die, I can be buried with the rest of the family in the Catholic section of the cemetery. Thank you.'

A moment of silence swept the congregation as everyone tried to process what she had said . . . then giggling and snorting erupted, filling the church. One or two of the staunch Catholics were clearly appalled. I saw Dad rolling his eyes.

I hid behind the baptismal font, hoping God was too busy to have heard Mum's embarrassing comment. Father Rufus had no choice but to continue with the baptism. He fingered Mum's forehead with oils and poured a tiny jug of water over it as she leaned over the font. I'm sure he would have preferred to have pushed her head right under the water and drowned her for blasphemy. He recited the necessary prayers, but the water was splashing everywhere because Mum wouldn't keep her head still; she was more concerned about her hair and make-up. By the time Father Rufus was finished with her, she looked like a crying clown.

To this day, I remain puzzled why Mum and Dad made such a fuss about being Catholic and spent such a fortune on sending us to Catholic schools. Neither of them ever stepped into a church other than for a marriage or a funeral. They never prayed, and we never said grace before meals. Being Catholic appeared to me to be a bit like the traditional male circumcision: you just do it to be like your dad. No questioning, no arguing, no debating. Simply cut it off, be Catholic and shut up. Amen.

Part XII

The Runaway Mother

'Brett! Get in the car! I'm leaving your fucking father!'

That was the best thing I ever heard as a child. . . and still brings a smile to my face when I think about it.

My mother screamed this declaration, at the top of her voice, outside my best friend's house when I was eleven years old, and her words were music to my ears. The idea of escaping my abusive, alcoholic father was a dream come true. I guess she had finally had enough. I mean, make-up can only conceal the bruises so much, and you can only kick a loyal dog so many times before it decides to walk away. Mum had now been kicked enough to reach her limit.

I was so excited about moving and starting a new life that I didn't give a second thought to saying goodbye to the best friend I was playing with at the time. I dropped everything, sprinted to the white Ford Falcon and jumped in. Mum sat in the driver's seat, wearing a floral frock, sandals and a black eye.

I stared at her with a huge Donny Osmond smile on my face; I was going to be her copilot on this new adventure! 'C'mon, Mum! Let's go!'

We drove off. My head was spinning with the kind of images of freedom that prisoners would have the night before they were released. We sang along with the radio, off on a magical adventure like Chitty Chitty Bang Bang.

Mum was going to become Mary Richards from the *Mary Tyler Moore Show*, which was my favourite sitcom at the time. Like Mary, she would navigate a new life in the big city, and I would tag along and enjoy our new happy life. I would become a citizen of the world. There would be exotic new food – far more options than the typical Aussie meals I had been used to. I was so elated I was hallucinating. I saw my life flashing before my eyes. I was heading to the metropolis, where I would see lots of musicals and attend a performing arts school. Perhaps I would even get on the telly; I set my sights on *Young Talent Time*, a television variety program where kids could sing and dance their hearts out. I would go shopping in the city with Mum and spend my Sundays at the beach with my new city friends, Tiffany and Coco. Every day would be a song and dance number, and all my dreams would come true.

Mum and I were delirious, sharing all the exciting things we could do living in a lovely big city on the coast. My imagination was running so wild, it took me ages before I realised she was driving aimlessly around town rather than heading towards Highway A32 to Adelaide. I assumed she was taking one last long look at the dusty mining town. We drove up and down all the streets in our suburb, south Broken Hill – streets so wide you could use them as aircraft landing strips. That was especially true of Knox Street, where Mum's best friend, Dotti, lived. It was like an international airport's main runway. Some of these vast streets had shade-giving eucalyptus trees along the footpaths, but most were asphalt roads lined with strong ironbark poles to support the power lines. Very ugly.

Mum eventually left our suburb and drove across the huge overpass that covers the railroad and divides the south of Broken Hill from the city centre and the rest of town. We continued to Argent Street, the main street. Being a mining town, many of the street names were named after rocks and minerals. So there was Cobalt Street, Crystal Street and Beryl Street; you would also find Chloride, Galena, Mercury and Mica Streets. If you ever decide to live there, you could find your next lovely home in Talc, Tin or Slag Street (it's not what you're thinking; slag is a term for scrap metal). Between each street are lanes that separate the rows of houses and allow access to their backyards. Each lane is usually named after the street parallel to it – so you would have Crystal Street followed by Crystal Lane, then Beryl Street followed by

Beryl Lane. Strangely enough, the town has a Lane Street which is followed by . . . yes, you guessed it: Lane Lane.

Mum's farewell tour of the town seemed to be taking ages, and I started to get anxious. We saw all the well-known landmarks of the place, like the Post Office building and the Palace Hotel in Argent Street, as well as the huge heap of slag metal waste that bisects the city, called the Line of Lode. It resembled a huge monolith, like the bright red one in the middle of Australia called Uluru / Ayers Rock; however, our town's monolith wasn't quite so stunning. It was and still is a heap of dirt left over from mining. It's lifeless and it looks burnt. In fact, it looks like the landscape on the moon. We passed by my high school, Willyama, which looks like a massive Mesopotamian ziggurat – a building with hardly any windows that was designed to prevent kids from being distracted by the outside world during lessons. That didn't work, as I discovered during my couple of years there.

We drove past many of the poppet heads dotted around the edges of the city. These are towering metal frameworks that cover the mine shafts; they have huge wheels at the top, part of the winding mechanism to transport the miners in a cage down into the earth. All these familiar images were now becoming part of our mental souvenir scrapbook as we embarked on this new adventure together.

Mum finally headed down Rakow Street – the road that led to the highway to freedom. My heart was pounding. We passed the sprawling cemetery, which is the last thing you see as you leave Broken Hill and the first thing you see when you enter. An enormous cemetery isn't the most welcoming image to be greeted by as you enter a city. I'm not sure what the local council members were thinking during their city planning. However, I guess seeing rows and rows of gravestones as you exit the place is a strong reminder to drive carefully.

Mum was driving carefully. But out of the blue, as we were passing the cemetery, she took a sharp left into Creedon Street, drove through the suburb of Railwaytown and recrossed the overpass, heading towards our home on the south side of town. Instead of taking the road to Adelaide, she took the road back to hell. I was mortified.

'Mum, what are you doing? I thought we were going to Adelaide?'

Mum couldn't look me in the face. She looked riddled with guilt and was choking on her tears.

'Turn around! We have to get out of here. Mum! Mum! We've got to go to Adelaide!'

After some deathly silence, she replied. 'Sorry, love, I've got to get home to make your father's tea.' She sounded utterly defeated.

Reality had slapped Mum in the face – and I wanted to do the same.

Part XIII

City Cousins

1. Country Mice and City Mice

My grandparents and cousins on my mother's side all lived in Adelaide. It's a very quiet city compared to Sydney or Melbourne, but rich in arts and culture; it's also culturally diverse, very relaxed and has hills and a beach. My mother grew up and briefly worked there before Dad literally swept her off her feet and plonked her in his own backyard. Every Christmas the family would alternate the trips. One year we country mice would head to Adelaide to spend the summer break with our cousins, then the following Christmas the city mice would pack their car to the brim with Christmas presents, luggage and my grandparents, say a prayer for their survival and head north into the desert to Broken Hill. My family were always full of excitement heading to a city full of adventure with so many fun things to do. I cannot imagine how my cousins felt packing the car for a four-week holiday in the dust and scorching heat. Either this represented a deep family loyalty, or they had a serious holiday obsession disorder.

When my family would head to Adelaide, we first visited our grandparents, Nanna and Pa. They could see how much we had grown, as well as Mum's latest bruises (despite her efforts to cover them up). We would always arrive at some ungodly hour in the morning, wake Nanna and Pa up and all sit on the edge of their bed, catching up on a year's worth of gossip. Nanna would always be sitting up with her hair in curlers, a scarf holding them in. Pa would be in his striped pyjamas with his top button done up and reading glasses perched on the edge of his huge nose. Nanna was a tough woman, eccentric and loud. I inherited two of those characteristics. Pa was the antithesis of her, a very lean, quiet, gentle soul. We could hardly get a word out of him. Nanna wore the pants in that relationship.

When the sun started rising, it was a sign we all needed sleep. Nanna and Pa would doze off again, and Mum would unpack and head to bed. Dad would drive us kids around to my aunty and uncle's house close by – this was a dream to us, like visiting Disneyland. My Aunty Madge and Uncle Arthur were hedonists who enjoyed the pleasures of life, especially when it came to food, drink and social gatherings. They loved to travel, watch endless hours of sport on TV and do cryptic crosswords. Aunty Madge and Uncle Arthur, together with their two kids, Billy and Mandy, were always fun to be with. Their house had a pool table, table tennis and a swimming pool. We would always eat exotic food like chicken noodle soup and drink coffee with lots of sugar, as well as gallons of Coke. Their television was always on and it had numerous channels to choose from, unlike the two channels – the conservative ABC Channel Two and the commercial Channel Seven – we had back in Broken Hill. Just jumping in the car with Aunty Madge to get the groceries was a real treat, as all the shops were different and new, offering a variety of things I didn't recognise. For four glorious weeks, we would stay with Madge and Arthur, eating desserts and doing loads of fun activities. Then we would pack up and head back to the desert, feeling depressed, anxious and irritable, but these mood swings weren't from the farewells and sad goodbyes; they were the unmistakeable symptoms of massive sugar withdrawal. I would be grumpy all the way home and end up in a dental chair a few months later, having my cavities inspected. Still, the mouthful of silver amalgam and mercury was worth it.

2. The Sem Tree Park

One of my favourite earliest memories of our trips to the beautiful city of Adelaide is of being a preschooler, around four or five years old, playing in a massive green park called the Sem Tree. It was the biggest park I had ever seen. Soon after we arrived in the city, the whole family would gather at Nanna's and Pa's house, where we would all cram into a couple of cars and head to the hills. Coming from the desert, entering the gates to this huge park felt like entering utopia. Once we had parked, the adults would gather and do whatever adults do and the kids would throw off their shoes and run madly around the vast space that was filled with tiny structures and statues of all different colours that looked like tree stumps. They were the perfect size for climbing and playing hide-and-seek. I remember running around endlessly, chasing my brothers and cousins, playing tag and hiding. There were flowers everywhere, as well. It was so pretty. There weren't any swings like in the parks back home – but it didn't matter; the space and all the lawn made up for it. It was such a treat to feel soft green grass beneath my tiny feet instead of hot sand and prickles.

Like most little kids having fun, I was totally oblivious to what the adults were doing. Every now and then, as my little legs ran all over the green grounds, I would stop to check where the family was, to keep my bearings and not get lost. They always seemed to be gathered in small groups or in pairs, but stationed in one area. I found it odd that they weren't keen to run around and explore the park like the kids.

Nevertheless, we kids always loved visiting the Sem Tree. Whenever I heard the name, I was like Pavlov's dog: my ears would prick up, my eyes widened and a rush of joy would fill my body as I knew I was in for a good time with my brothers and cousins. We filled every minute of the hour we were there playing and exploring. I was always disappointed when I heard Dad blow the car horn as a signal for all of us tots and scallywags to return immediately to the grown-ups. It meant our fun in the park was over and we were heading off to a boring place for grown-ups. But we always took family photos in the park before we left, and always at the same spot.

We visited that park each time we were in Adelaide. It didn't dawn on me until I got older that it wasn't a park called Sem Tree after all; it was the largest inner-city graveyard in Adelaide. As a toddler, I had no concept of a burial ground. I thought the grown-ups were saying, 'Right, in the car, we're going to the Sem Tree' – whereas they were actually saying 'cemetery' rather poorly. Those tiny structures and monuments were, of course, tombstones and the pretty flowers everywhere weren't permanent. The adults were gathering together to visit the grave of my cousin Chris, who tragically was shot at the young age of thirteen by a couple of teenagers in the neighbourhood. Apparently he and his brother were playing footy in their backyard when the football went over the fence. Chris climbed the fence to get it. A teenager next door was playing around with a gun, saw the intruder and decided to shoot just to frighten him, fully intending to miss. But he didn't miss; he shot him in the stomach. Chris's younger brother, Billy, saw the whole thing and just screamed. Another neighbour called the ambulance, and Chris was rushed to hospital. Sadly, he died on the way. I believe the teenager who shot the gun got it from his dad, who was a policeman. When the case went to court, he didn't get charged. He was too young.

Chris is now lying peacefully in the Sem Tree.

3. Jack the Clipper

As soon as the crow eaters (a term we call people from South Australia) had unpacked the car, Uncle Arthur would shout, 'C'mon, Brett – time to cut my hair!'

Now there's a risk-taker for you. I was only twelve years old, and he trusted me to give him his annual haircut. Not sure where he got the idea I had the skills of a barber, when really the only things I ever cut with scissors were my nails and the fabric for my periodic sewing bees. Actually, I lie; in mid-December you would also find me doing some scissor craft, cutting out snowflakes to decorate our silver tinsel Christmas tree. Anyhow, who was I to question? I would grab any scissors I could find, together with Mum's teasing comb, a chair and a towel. We would head outside and sit in the stinking hot dusty backyard. My little cousin Mandy would sit on the back step with her dolls, looking up every now and then to gape speechlessly as her dad's head was violated, his thick, black curly hair falling to the ground. Against the bright red sand, my uncle's hair looked like small desert rodents gathering around his feet.

I really had no idea what I was doing. I would try hard to remember the hand movements and snipping techniques of all the hairdressers and barbers who had cut my locks over the years. Now and then I would stand back like a sculptor admiring his masterpiece. But basically I was hacking into the poor man's head like Edward Scissorhands; I only stopped butchering his hair when I saw scalp. My skinny arms would ache and I'd often let out a little sigh of exhaustion, but Uncle Arthur would egg me on, saying, 'It's OK, just cut it. It's only hair, and it'll grow back.' True enough. They say there's only a week's difference between a good haircut and a bad one; Uncle Arthur had a good four weeks' annual leave up his sleeve over Christmas, so he was safe with me annihilating his hair. Nevertheless, he was always happy and seemed relieved to have his hair trimmed. I'm pretty sure he was just relieved to be saving five dollars on a haircut.

Uncle Arthur was a lovely man, always chirpy, positive and friendly to everyone. He would always compliment me on a job well done. I would have moments of fantasy about owning my own hairdressing business – 'Super Snips', 'Close Cuts' or 'Knock, Knock, Whose Hair?' However, from where I was standing, I knew my days as a hairdresser were numbered and I would be better off sticking to cutting fabric and making snowflakes.

Part XIV

Mum, the Nurse

In Broken Hill, married women were banned from working until the late 1970s. This was a union decree to protect young single people and provide these youngsters with employment, but even then I thought it was rather discriminating. Why didn't the rule apply to men as well? The idea was that they went to work, while the married women needed to stay home, have kids, look after them and run the household. I do understand it was a way of keeping a tiny economy running smoothly, but it was definitely not the best way to utilise everyone's skills and talents for the common good. So many talented, intelligent and creative women were forced to replace exciting careers with breastfeeding, vacuum cleaning and baking cakes.

Unionism was very strong in many mining towns globally, to protect the miners and improve their working conditions. That's always a good thing, but when it spilled over to the general community, I did wonder about the control it had and the abuse it administered. To me, I perceived it as a form of socialism. Still not sure if that was a good or a bad thing . . .

When the ban on women working was lifted in the mid-1970s, I was around thirteen or fourteen years old. It had been comforting and reassuring having my mother home all the time, but Mum couldn't get out of the house to look for a job quickly enough. She got lucky and secured a full-time position as a nursing assistant and cook in an aged care facility called St Agatha's. I guess converting to Catholicism finally paid off.

St Agatha's was owned by the Catholic Church, and half of the staff were nuns. For most of the elderly residents, the facility was a waiting room for heaven. Some of them had chronic illnesses that required twenty-four-hour care; others were suffering from Alzheimer's and other forms of dementia. Mum was thrilled to be out of the house and doing something different. A social moth, not quite as refined as a social butterfly, she loved being independent and meeting new people. She also loved earning her own money. We suddenly saw changes in the house: new curtains, bedspreads and carpet, and a huge double-doored fridge with a massive freezer suddenly adorning the kitchen. The kids started getting pocket money, which never came our way from Dad. We were thrilled. However, Mum was more thrilled than anyone; having her own income also meant a whole new addition to her wardrobe with blue uniforms, a range of new white shoes and tiny, cute nurse's hats. She always took pride in dressing up and now the nurse and chef regalia gave her an extra edge. It made her feel valued.

It wasn't all good, though. While Mum was pursuing her career and socialising all the time with her new colleagues, things were suffering on the home front – the meals in particular. We saw a big shift from home cooking to ready-made meals from the frozen section at the new Star Discount Supermarket in Patton Street. Worse still, Mum would often bring home leftovers of whatever she had been dishing up at St Agatha's. These so-called meals looked like blobs. The blobs came in three varieties – green, brown and white – and they were always smeared in gravy. Mum told us they were nutritious, texture-modified meals for people who had difficulty swallowing. We certainly had difficulty swallowing them.

I was convinced there was a blurred line between Mum's working days and her home life. Many evenings I would see her walk through the front door and head to our kitchen, still fully decked out in her uniform and nurse's hat, to prepare meals for her favourite residents: her family. She must have been in overdrive from work. Her failure to change her clothes meant the kitchen would suddenly have the unmistakable smell of a nursing home, a mixture of old people and the strong and unwanted scent of urine. We eventually got used to that, but we would never get used to some of those nursing home meals she dished up. We endured the three miniature pies with sauce, but drew the line at the poached egg floating in a bowl of milk. On a good night, Dad would throw the dish in the sink, swear, grab his keys and head for the pub. On a bad one, he would throw the dish at Mum.

Mum continued working at St Agatha's for years, and we all lost weight. During those years, she was the happiest I have ever seen her; the job gave her a sense of purpose and she loved mixing with people. She lived for her weekly hairdressing appointments, buying the latest fashions, and getting yet more shoes. She couldn't wait for the weekend, for her 'nights out with the girls'. They would head to the local clubs on a Saturday evening for a cabaret show and dancing. She loved having her own money – not least because it put the wind up Dad and made him think twice about abusing her, as she now had the freedom and finances to fly the coop whenever she wanted.

Even though Mum loved her job at the nursing home, she would often depress us during dinner with her endless stories about how the elderly were neglected or poorly treated. She had witnessed nurses thumping residents if they didn't comply, seen old people sitting in their own urine and faeces for hours because of understaffing, and heard staff members screaming and shaming residents out of mere frustration and exhaustion. Mum would always finish her stories with the same declaration: 'Don't you ever put me in that bloody home when I'm old. I'd rather you take me out the back and shoot me.' Well, we'd got rid of the gun after David shot Sandy, so we were really only left with one other option.

Mum is now a resident in the high-security ward of St Agatha's, as she suffers from dementia. Her poor memory means she no longer remembers who I am, but fortunately she can't remember ever working there either. I can only hope those awful memories are never triggered as she slurps down that floating poached egg in warm milk.

Part XV

Hot Santa

1. Christmas Down Under

When I think of Christmas time in Australia, I immediately have images of scorching heat, summer holidays and sunburn. It might seem strange to some of our northern hemisphere neighbours, who connect Christmas with snow, drinking warm mulled wine and ice skating – but you tend to accept whatever you grow up with as 'normal'. However, I have to admit that Mum painting snowflakes on the windows in the middle of summer didn't seem normal to me; in fact, it was a little weird. And having to wear a thick woollen costume to entertain the kids must have been torture for poor old Santa in the sweltering heat. Honestly, I don't think we really cared that none of it made sense. It was the holidays, we got presents, there was lots of food and it was fun – most of the time.

Most of the Christmases I experienced as a kid were at 45°C (113°F). It was fucking hot. We had a pitiful evaporative air cooler in the living room; you had to stand right in front of it to feel anything, and so our house was virtually an oven. It would lead anyone to drink. Christmas Down Under was simply an excuse to party, drink loads of alcohol and be constantly merry. I often wonder what Jesus would think of Christmas today. He must be weeping.

When you drove into town to do your Christmas shopping, you tried desperately to find a parking space under a tree or in some shade, or you wouldn't be able to get back into the car without passing out from the heat. It was like sticking your head in a kiln. To prevent burning your thighs, it was common to place bath towels over the vinyl car seats. Once you forced yourself into the driver's seat – because you had to get that butter and bucket of ice-cream home into the fridge fast – you had to bear the pain of touching the steering wheel and gearstick, which were searing hot.

You would start the car and turn the air conditioner on full blast, and then time would stand still while you waited for it to kick in and reach a temperature that would cool the interior of the car down, as well as your face. It invariably got there just as you turned into your driveway. And when you got home, you would need to scrape the black gunk off your shoes from when you'd walked across the bubbling asphalt in the car park; the heat was so intense it would melt the tar. I even once saw a neighbour fry an egg on the hood of his car (or maybe he used his neighbour's car so he didn't risk scratching the hell out of his own paintwork). I was so tempted to try French toast and scrambled eggs on Dad's car, his pride and joy. I wish I had.

2. Father Christmas

I do recall being very excited as a kid about the jolly fat man in his red suit. Even though the notion of a man flying around the world in a sleigh pulled by reindeer is ridiculous and humanly impossible, it appealed to my wild imagination. It was also exciting to think I could turn up to the shopping centre, sit on Santa's knee for a few minutes, tell him what I wanted for Christmas, and it would miraculously appear under the cheap tinsel tree in our living room one special morning. Amazing. But I had no reason not to believe; Santa was surely as real as the Tooth Fairy and the Easter Bunny.

It was all very enticing, but it did feel a little weird sitting on this elderly stranger's leg, having snapshots taken. Even weirder that Mum and Dad – usually obsessed with having security screens and locked doors on the house – would let this stranger in a red suit sneak into our home in the middle of the night. He would wander around the place, drop off some gifts, gobble up the food, and drink the cold beer we left for him. I was amazed he did this in every house in the world; no wonder he was fat. And what about the drinking and driving issue?

But one day my world was shattered. We can all recall the moment we discovered Santa wasn't real, right? In my case, 'twas the night before Christmas. I was about seven or eight years old and had been helping Mum put out plates of food for Santa and the reindeer, as well as a cold bottle of beer for him, since it was such a hot evening. My relatives from Adelaide were visiting and the grown-ups were settled into the living room, watching TV. Mum and Dad had threatened me and my brothers that if we didn't get to bed early, we were not to expect any presents under the Christmas tree next morning. That kind of bribe always worked. So off to bed we eventually went.

However, I awoke around midnight from all the loud chatter and noise coming from the grown-ups in the living room. It crossed my mind that perhaps they were excited and chatting to Santa. I couldn't resist; I had to jump out of bed and take a peek at the man himself putting all the presents under the tree and enjoying the food and drink we'd left him. First, I peeked through the bedroom curtains on the off chance of seeing the magical sleigh and reindeer in the front garden, as I hadn't heard them land on the roof. Nothing. So I softly crept up the passage towards the living room. Very carefully, I stretched up to grab the door handle and opened the door a little to poke my nose and one eye through the gap, to see what all the raucous laughter was about.

I was horrified, and my heart was crushed.

There was no Father Christmas. Instead, there was my father drinking Santa's beer, and everyone else scoffing his food. What was worse was seeing my mum and aunty on the living room floor wrapping presents, sticking name tags on them and placing them under the Christmas tree. Santa didn't deliver them? What a rip-off. I was so confused and upset I went straight to my big brother, Mick, in the other bedroom and woke him up.

'Mick, Dad is drinking Santa's beer and Mum is wrapping presents. Where is Santa?'

My brother didn't even move his head or open his eyes. He just mumbled, 'There is no Santa, dickhead.'

My other older brother, David, also woke up and decided to contribute to crushing my childhood fantasies. 'Yeah, and there's also no such thing as a Tooth Fairy, Easter Bunny, monsters or bogeyman. Now shut up and go back to bed.'

My jaw dropped. I ran to my bed and cried into my pillow. In fact, I cried all summer.

3. Christmas Surprise

My grandfather Jack, Dad's father, whom I adored because he was so funny and talented, lived in the centre of town with his son Clare, Dad's brother. Jack had wild white hair and a big stomach like Santa's, a wrinkly face that looked like a fingerprint, and about five teeth in total. He would visit us from time to time – mostly around mealtimes – and entertain us all with hilarious stories and jokes. Despite being poor, he never turned up empty-handed; however, given the things he brought, it was clear he just cleaned out his cupboards or his dusty shed. It was mostly junk. There were old suitcases that wouldn't close, shoes that had seen better days, a rusted bike with no seat or chain, an old toaster with no plug attached. Everything Jack brought out had to be fixed in some way, or it was of no use at all. He once brought Mum a corset. Bless his heart, he thought she'd be thrilled. She never had the balls to tell him corsets hadn't been worn since the 1920s, so he really should have placed it in the local museum. Instead, Mum placed it in the trash after he had left.

We didn't really mind Jack bringing out all his junk; he was a gentle soul who liked to lift people's spirits and help them out wherever he could. He was a man with a good heart – or so we thought. One Christmas morning he surprised us with a visit, right before lunch. As usual, he had done his spring cleaning and brought some junk for us as Christmas gifts. He also gave each of us a copper penny. But on this particular day, Jack didn't look like his usual perky self. In fact, he looked lost and tired.

Even though the house was full with the family visiting from Adelaide, Mum insisted Jack stay for Christmas lunch, which was always a feast. I never saw anyone say yes so quickly. I had also never seen Grandpa Jack at our Christmas lunch before – he would normally visit Dad's other brothers – so it was a nice change having him around. Dad handed him a cold beer and offered him a chair. Grandpa sat back and entertained us with his funny stories and jokes.

Out of guilt, Mum grabbed a present from under the tree that she had been planning on giving to Pa, her own dad. She ripped off the name tag and gave it to Grandpa Jack instead, wishing him a merry Christmas. He was surprised and seemed very touched by the gesture. He was even more surprised when he opened it to find a silk tie and a tiepin, because the last time he'd ever worn either was at his own wedding, fifty years earlier. Now he only wore white singlets. Still, the thought was there. I'm sure Mum believed that within a couple of months Jack would forget who had given it to him, and the gift would come back to us along with another corset or some worn-out shoes.

Mum and Aunty Madge always spent the entire morning preparing the big feed, with all the traditional English Christmas dishes: stuffed turkey, roast potatoes, stuffing, mince pies and Christmas pudding with hot custard. It never made sense to me that we would all sit down in the scorching heat to fill our stomachs with piping hot food. The kitchen was stifling from all the cooking, and we would all be sweating and gasping as we tried to gulp down all the hot, rich, fatty food.

We managed to get through it all, but by the end of it, we were more stuffed than the turkey. Nobody could move from all the bingeing and the expanded tummies. While poor Mum and her sister-in-law cleaned everything up, all the men and the kids rolled into the lounge room to get some oxygen and a bit of relief in front of the air cooler, perching themselves in one spot to watch endless cricket matches on TV all afternoon.

Grandpa Jack was so full, he found it painful even to sit down, so he decided to go for a walk around the block to fart and belch it all out, regardless of the sweltering heat. Jack invited us to join him, but we were all too bloated and lethargic; besides, there was no way we were going to head out into the midday sun. Nothing would budge us from the air cooler. Jack waddled outside, shouting that he would be back soon – it would only be a quick walk around the block.

Well, it was quick, but he never made it back. Halfway round, he had a heart attack, collapsed and died in the street. He may have had a kind heart, but he didn't have a healthy one.

Grandpa Jack dying on Christmas Day suddenly took the merry out of Merry Christmas. We all went from being filled with joy and good cheer to feeling depressed. We had been planning to have a Christmas dinner with all the leftovers from lunch, but we suddenly lost our appetites. Instead of drinking and celebrating, we spent the rest of the day contacting relatives and grieving. We didn't expect Jack to die so suddenly.

We also didn't expect to see the silk tie and pin back so swiftly. Fortunately, we didn't have to worry about getting a refund; Mum just rewrapped them. She replaced the old tag and popped the gift back under the Christmas tree for my Pa – the sole surviving grandfather.

Part XVI

Dancing Lessons

1. Dancing Queen

In elementary school, my best friend was Ricky. I used to love staying and playing at his house every week, and we did everything together. Sadly, he lost his dad when he was very young, leaving him with his mum, two older sisters and a younger brother. When I was about nine years old, his older sister Libby was about twenty-five. She ran a ballroom dancing school and was desperate for boys to join so the girls didn't have to always dance with each other. Ricky signed up out of familial loyalty and persuaded me to join too. Ricky only lasted two lessons and then left, but I took to it like a duck to water. I was hooked.

Even though my brothers believed learning to dance was a very girly thing to do, I learnt how to ask girls to be my partner on the dance floor, something my brothers were never good at; they preferred aggressive activities like football and boxing. Whenever I played those sports, I was like a ship without a harbour. They weren't my thing. Ballroom dancing, though, was perfect for me. Apart from the wonderful variety of music, the exciting challenge of conquering intricate steps and wearing fabulous costumes, dancing built my confidence and gave me another way to express myself creatively. Flinging my arms, doing kick ball changes and graceful slides with my partner was a weekly thrill.

Libby's School of Ballroom Dancing became one of my favourite haunts, and I could be found there every Thursday evening. Libby matched me up with a sweet girl, Sissy Townsend. Her mother would pick me up every Thursday evening in her white Volkswagen and drop us both off at the dance hall in Crystal Street for our private lessons. We learnt modern, Latin and old-time ballroom dances: foxtrot, quickstep, waltz, cha-cha-cha, rumba, gypsy tap and jive. My favourites were always the Latin dances because they were fast, lively and energetic – and because when we had to perform them in local clubs, these dances meant wearing colourful silky shirts, bright cummerbunds, glittering tops, waistcoats and colourful bow ties. Of course, my outfits were nothing compared with the spectacular sparkly dresses Sissy got to wear, with their yards of colourful tulle, feathers and sequins. I was so envious. However, I was still beside myself with my costumes. They made me and my wardrobe come alive.

I made Mum buy me every ballroom dancing record available in the music stores and I would play them endlessly, dancing around in the living room, sometimes with an imaginary partner or with Mum; she was a Dancing Queen too. She spent a lot of time dancing when she was a child and often performed on stage, and as an adult, she loved to go dancing in the local clubs every weekend, so she supported me wholeheartedly. I think she was counting on me replacing Dad as her partner at the club one day, as she was getting sick and tired of pushing a drunk around the dance floor. Mum was still dancing right up to the day she danced her way into a nursing home. Even though she now suffers from severe dementia and can't remember if she brushed her teeth, the nurses tell me Mum gets excited as soon as music is played. She gets up and dances around the ward, down memory lane, never forgetting a step. Such joy.

Dancing brought such joy to me as well. Sissy and I were partners for years. Our teacher, Libby, had a lot of faith in us and was proud to show us off to the community with every chance she got. She would book us regularly to perform at clubs and special events. She said it would be good for us, which was true, but it was also really good for business; it was free advertising for Libby's School of Ballroom Dancing. But we really didn't care. We both loved dressing up and performing. We felt like stars when the lights went down and the spotlight was on us. Once the music started, we were in cha-cha heaven.

2. Shall We Dance?

Sissy and I were getting very good at dancing together, and we looked forward to it every week. The thing about dancing with a partner regularly for a few years is that the two of you develop a special connection. It's as if you're learning to listen and speak at the same time; it's a two-way conversation in which you have to listen to what your partner's body is saying while yours speaks. Your partner follows the way you move your body and the way they follow you feeds back into how you lead. It takes a long time to feel that connection with a partner, but when it happens, it's magic. I always felt the same when I danced with my mother. She was brilliant at listening to her dance partners and striking up a dance conversation, without talking. I got to know all Mum's favourite dance movements, and we would glide effortlessly around the dance floor. We weren't quite Fred Astaire and Ginger Rogers, but we could make people watch in awe; she revelled in that.

Libby decided Sissy and I needed to step it up a notch, so she sent us off to Adelaide to dance competitively. Sissy, her mum and I packed our lovely costumes and hairspray and caught a bus to the big city. We made a weekend of it. We booked into the Plaza Hotel, close to the dance venue – it sounds posh, but was actually a dirt-cheap dive on Hindley Street, at the sleazy side of the city centre. So cheap that it had no air conditioning, the place was blistering hot. In the middle of the pitch-dark night, I crawled towards the closed curtains, pulled them apart and felt the hung sash window. The frame was stiff, but I managed to lift it up to let some air into the room. I sat near the window for a moment, feeling a slight breeze. *Aaah, that's better.* I felt much cooler, so I headed back to bed and settled down for the night.

Next morning, I was shocked to find there was no opening in the window at all; it was totally bricked in. It's amazing what the mind can do.

Sissy and I spent the whole morning dressing up, doing our hair and make-up and practising our steps in the tiny hotel room. We headed to the nearby dance studio and signed in. There was a judges' table on one side of the room and a sound system on the other. Two huge chandeliers hung from the ceiling. There were many clones of us, all about the same age, all standing around the edge of the room stretching and getting some last-minute practice steps in, all looking very highly strung and stiff. Sissy and I weren't nervous at all. We loved the social side of ballroom dancing – it was all we knew. We really didn't care about the competitive side. It didn't make sense to us if it wasn't fun.

They announced the dances, and the couples all exploded onto the dance floor, taking their positions. It was a fantasy land: everything and everyone looked beautiful and glistened. Sissy and I went to the floor casually and danced as if we were in our little dance hall back home on Crystal Street. While everyone else had false smiles and fake attitudes, we giggled and mimicked our competitors. We knew we didn't stand a chance against these ferociously competitive prima donna ballroom dancers with their military postures, so we just relaxed and enjoyed ourselves. It was an interesting experience, but we knew competitive dancing wasn't going to be for us. We couldn't take it seriously. We preferred to have fun.

In fact, the most memorable part of that weekend away for me was going to the cinema together on the Saturday evening to watch Barbra Streisand in *Funny Girl*. It made me laugh, but despite my love of dancing, I didn't see myself as part of the Ziegfeld Follies like Fanny Brice, Barbra's character.

We had almost forgotten about the competition by the time we returned home – so it came as a complete surprise to us a couple of weeks later when the postman delivered us three bronze medals each, one for every section: Modern, Old Time and Latin. Those medals stood proudly on the living room mantelpiece above the fireplace for years, right next to all my brothers' huge football trophies.

Maybe my brothers were right – ballroom dancing may have been a girly thing to do. However, my brothers' performances as footballers were, unfortunately for them, very short-lived, while I have managed to dance my feet off through the decades. Watching my brothers doing their big first dances at their weddings was just too painful. They looked traumatised. They would have been better off replacing their embarrassing bridal shuffles with the Birdie Dance. A phone call to Libby could have done wonders. In case you are wondering – yes, my husband (also a ballroom medallist) and I performed a very creative waltz/jive combo bridal dance decades later at our own wedding party.

Learning to dance adds a magical dimension to one's life. It opens so many exciting opportunities. Every answer to the question 'Why do we dance?' would be different. Perhaps the better question would be 'Why would we not?'

Dancing has brought the greatest joy to me over many years, from dancing in my childhood with sweet Sissy to partnering with lovely ladies making their debuts. You could always find me tripping the light fantastic at discos. I have danced salsas in Ecuador and slow tangos in Amsterdam, and tap-danced my way through Tokyo. I have collected memorable moments dancing with my mother, including doing a jive with her in the dementia ward of St Agatha's. Bless her.

Part XVII

Piano Man

1. Out With the Old

I had eight years of torturous piano lessons with Sister Stephen (may she rest in peace). This meant a huge part of my childhood was spent practising scales, trying to play like Bach, Mozart, Beethoven or Chopin, and praying. I think Sister Stephen had high hopes of me becoming a classical pianist, or a Catholic priest, but I wasn't really cut out for either. I loved playing ABBA's music too much, and my exciting nocturnal emissions were enough to convince me that a life of celibacy was not part of God's plan or mine.

It was the mid-1970s – the decade of glam rock, heavy metal and disco – and I was so over classical music. I would spend hours at the local music store buying loads of sheet music so I could learn to play like Elton John, Benny Andersson or Barry Manilow. They were much more exciting than boring Bach. I wasn't sure why I was still playing and praying with Sister Stephen. So I plucked up the courage to speak to her honestly. I told her how I felt. I asked if I could stop learning the classical pieces and begged her to let me do something more modern.

Sister Stephen sat motionless, staring at Jesus, her husband, hanging on the cross above the piano. I suspected she was silently repeating the words Jesus said as he was dying on the cross: *Father, forgive him, for he knows not what he is doing.* I suspected she must have been shattered; she had wasted eight years of her life trying to train a classical music child prodigy, and he had just thrown it back in her face. What I do know is that she wasted her time making me pray all those years. I was now convinced God did not exist, but if there was a hell, I was already there.

Eventually, Sister Stephen sat up straight with her hands on her breasts (which were resting on her knees), let out a huge sigh and said, 'Fine.' She stood up and plodded over to her little wooden cabinet, pulled out a sheet of music and blew the dust off it, then ambled back to her seat, plonked the paper in front of me and said, 'There you go – the *Blue Danube*. It's a modern piece by Johann Strauss.'

It immediately became clear to me that 'modern' to Sister Stephen meant any time after the Middle Ages and that she obviously didn't own a radio or television.

Disappointed, I decided there and then that this would be my swansong. I played the music slowly and graciously, and did old Johann proud. When I played the final note, I turned slowly on my piano stool and stared coldly at the old nun. I forced a gentle smile, knowing full well this was going to be our final day together, and said, 'Thank you, Sister Stephen. May the Lord be with you, and the peace and blessings from God our Father and Lord Jesus Christ be forever upon you.' What I really wanted to say, of course, was, 'May the Lord forgive you, for you really have no bloody idea.' I grabbed my music books, said my goodbyes and left. Her mission was over, and so were my lessons.

2. Myste

Quitting piano lessons gave me a chance to play all the modern sheet music I bought from the local piano store: 'Stairway to Heaven', 'Ballroom Blitz', and every song by ABBA, the Beatles, Chicago and the Bee Gees. I finally had something different to play besides sonatas and polkas. Don't get me wrong – I appreciated classical tunes, but they weren't music to my teenage ears. I developed a huge repertoire of rock and disco tunes and had a huge desire to perform. To give Sister Stephen her due, she did teach me to be a great sight reader; I could pick up any piece of music and play it straight away.

As I read the local paper one Saturday morning, I came

across an advertisement for a professional cabaret band, Myste, looking for a piano player. I was only thirteen years old, but I thought, *This is it! It's now or never. I need to get on stage and entertain.* Jesus was a risk-taker, and so was I. We didn't have a phone at the time, so I wrote the number down and ran next door to Mrs Richards, promising that if she let me use the phone for a local call, I would wash her car. She agreed. Slave driver!

When I dialled the number to speak to Bernard, the band's main singer, I suddenly realised all the guys in the band were likely in their twenties and thirties. You had to be an adult to enter the local clubs, so I spoke as deeply as I could; desperate times called for desperate measures. Surprisingly, it worked and I scored an audition time the following Saturday afternoon. I was so excited I would have happily washed every car in the street.

The day arrived for the audition, and I had to work up the courage to ask Dad to drive me and take me into the local club, as I needed an adult to accompany me. Although he generally hated anything I did, when it came to music, he was one hundred percent behind me – perhaps because he and his brothers had also been those budding musicians when they were young. He probably saw in me the musician he had never quite managed to become.

I grabbed a pile of music and we headed for the club. We made it through to the huge auditorium, where all the band members of Myste were on stage with their instruments. A lonely Steinway baby grand piano stood in the corner. In front of the stage was a line of about ten pianists waiting patiently to audition for the band; they were all adults. I thought I wouldn't stand a chance to even audition, let alone score the job. I didn't care. I was driven by my passion, so I joined the line with Dad by my side.

Each performer had to play two of their favourite pieces and a very long piece of cabaret music given to them by the band. When they had finished, the band members clearly gave a code to Bernard and he would announce, 'Great.

Thank you. We will be in touch. Next!' When it came to my turn, the band thought Dad was the one auditioning. They called out to Dad, 'OK, you're next. What's your name?'

Dad swiftly replied, 'It's Kevin. But it's my kid, Brett, who's auditioning.'

The band broke out into laughter.

Bernard smiled. 'That's cute. Well, what the hell, it is the last audition. Come on up, kid, and give it a shot.'

I could see they were just being kind. They had to be; there's an unspoken bond and a deep respect between musicians, no matter what their age. Experienced musicians know all the years of pain and practice it takes to master an instrument, and they understand the need to always encourage each other to never give up, for the rewards are immeasurable. They knew turning me away from an audition as a kid could have shattered my musical dreams forever.

I jumped up on stage, sat at the piano and played 'Billy Don't Be a Hero' by Paper Lace and 'Waterloo' by ABBA. They were impressed. Next, they gave me the longest score I had ever seen, a piano accompaniment piece called 'Nobody Does It Like Me' by Shirley Bassey. I had never heard of the song, let alone her. What now sat before me looked like a long sheet with ants running all over it. If there was a God, I needed His help right at that moment.

There was no going back now. I quickly scanned it, took a deep breath and played every note I could see. Turning around when I'd finished, I could see the band looked dazzled. Bernard was chatting excitedly to the group as I grabbed my music and made my way down to Dad.

I saw Bernard walk over to the microphone and waited for the inevitable 'Great. Thank you. We will be in touch.'

Instead, he looked down, a huge smile on his face . . . and, to my astonishment, announced, 'Great. Thank you. You've got the job, kiddo.'

Now *that* was music to my ears.

3. Girls Just Want to Have Fun

How lucky was I to have scored a job with this band of adult professional musicians? We would rehearse every Saturday afternoon, learning all the latest hits. Sometimes we would act as a backing band, supporting special cabaret artists like Little Pattie and Debbie Byrne who had flown in from Sydney. I used to love that. It was exciting to meet celebrities; they added so much variety to a gig and were so entertaining. Playing all their very long piano accompaniment pieces was a challenge, but it was thrilling.

While my teenage peers spent Friday and Saturday nights making mischief, I spent most of my weekends at the local clubs performing with Myste and making good money. And it wasn't only the money that was great. The band members took me under their wings, teaching me dirty jokes and a lot about music. They would also take me on trips to Adelaide to see rock concerts: Electric Light Orchestra, Boz Scaggs, Slade and Status Quo. What a buzz. We would buy their music and then do our best to learn the songs for our local gigs.

Mum and her friend Dotti were my best fans. They would get dressed up and come to every club and gig Myste played. I would secure the table closest to the stage, and they would always be the first on the floor, together. There is nothing more deflating to a band than playing a set of songs with no one on the dance floor. But our band was so cool, with so many talented musicians, that the floor was always full. I would sit on stage at my piano, enjoying both the playing and the feeling of watching people enjoying our music. I was immensely grateful for the opportunity.

It was also interesting to watch an audience get drunker as the evening progressed. Their coordination would get worse, their dance steps out of sync, and quite a few would actually topple over. When they weren't dancing, they were screaming their lungs out trying to sing louder than the band. It was always a thrill to see people losing their minds and enjoying themselves.

I also saw some of the inevitable brawls and fights that came with a drunken crowd. One night I saw an argument brewing on the dance floor: two women who didn't have a set of teeth between them were shouting at each other, nudging and pushing until they were both completely enraged. I couldn't hear or work out what it was about, but I assumed there was some jealousy over the guy one of the women was dancing with. The jealous one had had enough and decided to put an end to it. She stormed over and, standing right behind the other woman, kicked the back of her victim's legs so hard that she instantly collapsed in a heap on the floor. Not satisfied, the perpetrator continued ramming kicks into the crumpled dancer while she was down on all fours. The weird thing about it all was that everyone around them just kept on dancing, and we kept on playing.

When the audience is having a good time – OK, when the audience is drunk – nothing can stop them. In fact, in my hometown they enjoy a brawl, especially between women. They regard it as an extra bit of unpaid-for entertainment and a sign of a good night out.

Part XVIII

Chucking Laps

In Australia, turning seventeen years of age is every teenager's dream because it's when we can get a driving licence. Simultaneously, it is every parent's nightmare. They know they will never see their car again, and their stress levels will rise as they lie awake at night, waiting for their child to pull safely back into the driveway. I guess they always remember how reckless they were when they got their licences.

Getting a licence is probably the first time a teenager experiences a real sense of freedom from their parents. It becomes a rite of passage that signifies you have gained some independence. Some kids at school were lucky to have well-to-do parents who bought them their own cars. Not me; my parents could barely afford one for themselves.

Nevertheless, I borrowed Mum and Dad's brand-new little blue Toyota Corolla every chance I could get, and I think I did more miles in a year than Mum and Dad did in their lifetime. I loved the freedom, and I didn't even mind jumping in the car to do errands or zipping up to the supermarket. Anything to just get in the car, turn the radio up, and cruise. Until then, I had usually been the one bumming a ride from my parents. But when the tables turn, and you actually have to pick up your parents from somewhere, there's a strange sense of satisfaction in being the chauffeur . . . that is, until they expect you to pay for the gas.

I couldn't wait to join all the other Engine Eddies and cruise down Argent Street, popping cassettes into the cassette deck and playing my favourite cruisin' tunes, singing along and waving to my friends, free and easy. It was tame compared with the kinds of things others did. Some lads would rev their cars and burn their tyres taking off fast from traffic lights, continually blowing their horns and shouting obscenities. Some of the girls I went to school with were just as bad, if not worse. One girl – well known around town as Godiva – often drove down the main street on a Friday night with nothing on but the radio.

We always remember our first solo drive after passing the test. My first trip was to pick up one of my best friends, Kathy; it was time to repay her for driving me all over town for months (she was a few months older, so got her licence earlier). Kathy is a very dear friend and one of the sweetest people you could ever meet. She has a huge Osmond smile and a big heart. Gentleness is at the core of her being. She is incredibly smart, has a brilliant sense of humour, loves to laugh and is the kind of friend everyone wants. I was incredibly lucky to meet her in high school, but we clicked and remained friends for life.

Does she have any faults? Yes. One is that she's so loving and forgiving, people can hurt her unintentionally. The other is that she made a couple of poor choices with her hairstyle. In our last year of school together, Kathy went through a perm phase, inspired by Barbra Streisand in *A Star Is Born*. Unlike Babs, though, Kathy had long hair. After leaving the salon with her new perm, she had to walk home in the rain without an umbrella. With every step she took, the gentle waves in her hair turned into an afro . . . and by the time she made it home, the curls were so tight that she looked like a lamb. She wore that afro proudly. Being a good friend, I decided to get my hair permed as well. However, I made sure the weather was fine.

Anyhow, Kathy came running out of her house, smiling broadly, full of joy. She jumped into the little blue Corolla and we drove off. We zipped around the corner to pick up Jenny, another good friend who also loved perms; hers was a red version. Coming from a middle-class background, Jenny was the posh one out of us three. Her civilised family ate fresh fruit salad, instead of fruit out of a can like Kathy and me. They lived in a brick house with a pretty garden and manicured lawns, in the more affluent area of Broken Hill. Her parents were very loving to each other and their kids. Kathy and I wanted them to adopt us.

Together, the three of us spent hours driving all over town, as if we were discovering the place for the very first time. It didn't take much to amuse us, but it was usually at the expense of others. Our favourite thing was this: driving down a quiet street, if we saw somebody walking along on one side of the street with no one else around, we would blow the horn to grab their attention but wave frantically to an imaginary person on the other side instead. We had no idea how it made the lone walker feel, but it had us laughing hysterically. We also enjoyed checking out churches to see if there were any weddings on. If the bride and groom were standing outside for photos, we would honk the horn loudly and wave, thinking we were adding to their special day . . . unlike some feral friends of ours, who would crawl past a bridal couple, wind the window down and shout, 'Fuck her – I did!' It must have made the bride feel very special.

I was very careful driving Dad's car, as it was his prized possession. My friend Kathy, on the other hand, had a slightly more relaxed attitude towards driving her dad's huge cream-coloured Ford Falcon. Whenever she was at the steering wheel, we knew we were in for some adventures. One Sunday, she picked Jenny and me up and we drove all over town trying to find streets and lanes we had never been down before. We took a tight, narrow lane that eventually turned into a dirt track. We ended up in the scrub behind the local drive-in cinema, which was really only fit for four-wheel drives or army tanks.

We had no idea where we were going. It didn't sound good, either; we could hear screeching and scratching and large rocks scraping under the car. When we finally found our way back to a sealed road, we jumped out of the car to check the damage. The dry, thorny mulga bushes and trees had scraped all the exterior duco, the tyres were covered in thorny prickles, and the vinyl covering on the roof had been ripped to shreds. It was totally covered in red dust as well. We had entered the scrub with a slick, shiny car and exited with a wreck on four wheels.

Her dad is going to kill her.

Kathy didn't seem to be too bothered about it, so we pressed on to our favourite local milk bar, Bell's, where everyone would end up on a hot Sunday afternoon for one of the best milkshakes in town. It was a classic Australian milk bar that had been around since 1892. It had a modern retro look with chrome fittings and 1950s furniture. The lady who ran it, Mrs Bell, was a real character with bright plastered make-up and a blonde bouffant hairdo, which was sometimes tinted pink or lime green. She sold old-style drinks, malted milkshakes and soda 'spiders' (a mix of homemade cordial, very fizzy soda, ice, and a large scoop of ice-cream) that had a real tang to them but were so refreshing. There were a variety of flavours – green lime, sarsaparilla, ginger beer and blue raspberry – but my favourite was creme and soda. Mrs Bell made all the special cordials and syrups for the milkshakes and spiders. They tasted out of this world. I was always curious about the ingredients and wondered how one drink could cause me to feel so high and so happy, but apparently the recipe was a secret. Mrs Bell would try to convince people it was probably the amount of sugar she was using. However, since she had the face of a sad clown and the smile of a crystal meth addict, you can't tell me those special drinks didn't have a teaspoon of illegality in them.

When the sugar (or whatever) crash hit and the sun was dropping lower, around 5:30 pm, it was tea time. It was always depressing heading home after such a fun adventure. We had driven for hours around town, causing mischief, and abusing the locals as well as the car. Kathy dropped me off home first. As she stopped the car in front of my house, Jenny and I noticed an unusual smell.

'Kathy, can you smell that?' I asked.

'What?'

'That strange smell,' added Jenny.

Kathy shrugged. 'Nope.'

I wound down the window. 'Yeah, take a big sniff. It smells like smoke or burning rubber?'

We all took a big snort.

'Really? . . . Oh, yeah, you're right. I can smell it too,' Kathy said curiously.

Jenny covered her nose. 'What is it? It's getting stronger.'

'Yeah, it smells really odd,' I added. 'Maybe the oil is leaking?'

'Oh, shit!' shouted Kathy.

'What? What is it?' said Jenny.

Kathy's face was turning bright red. 'I had the handbrake on the whole day!'

Jenny and I burst out laughing.

Her dad is definitely *going to kill her.*

Part XIX

Puberty Blues

1. What's Going on Down Under?

The teenage years are often a very weird time. You feel like you're constantly fighting an inner battle, straddling childhood and adulthood. I felt like a kid in a grown-up body; my brain was still imagining, creating and clowning around, while my body was raging with sex, stress and growth hormones. Everyone, especially parents, expected me to be all grown up, but deep down all I wanted to do was go outside and play with my friends, figuratively and literally.

Being a teenager meant facing many new challenges. I had to deal with my first pimple, my first erection and the sprouting of my first pubic hair, as well as my first kiss, crush, and heartbreak. My first orgasm was a wet dream. I wasn't prepared for that. I woke up in the middle of the night all wet and sticky and thought something was terribly wrong . . . yet it felt so terribly good.

My strict Catholic school offered no sex education whatsoever; when we were ten years old, they only gave us all a little green book written by the local parish priest that was supposed to tell us everything. It did have a labelled diagram, so I could finally learn the correct names for my genitalia, but when it came to the birds and the bees and how babies were made, it was all about the Virgin Mary and her immaculate conception. It was very confusing, and I really couldn't see how I had a role in the whole process at all. I was waiting for Mum and Dad to tell me about the real facts of life, but when they had spent years calling my genitals winky, pee-pee and doody, I knew it wasn't going to happen. If they were too embarrassed to say 'penis', there was no way we would be sitting down for a good old chat about doing the dipsy doodle.

I just had to work it all out by myself.

I spent my first year of high school at a public school called Willyama High, because one of my best friends, Ricky (the younger brother of the ballroom dancing teacher), had decided to go there. But it was on the other side of town and too far from my weekly piano lessons at the convent, so Mum and Dad made me return to the Catholic school the following year. I was back with the kids from my elementary school days. It was so great seeing their familiar faces – even though they were all now covered in acne and fuzz. I arrived late on the first day, and when I got to the classroom the teacher – Brother Aaron, a Marist Brother – told me to go to the back of the room and take the spare seat at a desk next to a very pretty girl. She struck up a welcoming conversation.

'Hi, I'm Lea.'

'Hi, I'm Brett.'

'Welcome to St Joseph's.'

'Thanks.'

'I have a question for you, Brett.'

'Sure, Lea. What is it?'

'Does a penis have a bone in it?'

'Seriously?'

'Yes.'

'Of course it doesn't.'

'Can you show me?'

'Well, I'll show you mine if you show me yours.'

'But I don't have a penis.'

We both burst out laughing. This school looked like it would be fun. However, that all changed when Brother Aaron kept us in during lunch recess for disturbing the lesson.

2. Sucking Face

My first real 'pash' or 'snog' with a girl was in a movie house when I was around thirteen years old. We had a local movie theatre in Oxide Street, the Silver City Cinema. It was built in 1964 and it was huge, with split-level seating and over five hundred seats. It had a thriving candy bar and loads of films for kids and teenagers, so it was the place to hang out. This was, of course, a time before videos and Netflix came on the scene, so it was very popular and always packed to the rafters. You could always turn up to the cinema alone and be guaranteed to end up sitting with someone you knew. Many people would have experienced their first kiss in that place, their feet getting crushed as people shuffled past, or hair being tangled with chewing gum from the halfwit behind them who planted it on their head for a dare.

I went to the cinema with a schoolmate, Chris, one Friday evening to see *The Apple Dumpling Gang*. Chris was a good-looking guy and very popular with all the girls. We sat in the dark directly behind two girls Chris knew, Samantha and Fiona. The film was boring, so Chris thought we should chat them up, especially as he had the hots for Samantha. He leaned forward, tapped her on the shoulder and started up a conversation.

'How ya goin'?'

The girls were surprised but keen to chat; they apparently found the film as boring as we did.

Samantha appeared to be drooling. 'Hey, Chris. Would you like some of my popcorn?'

'Thanks.' Chris grabbed a handful of popcorn. 'Boring film, hey?'

Fiona turned her whole body around to join in the conversation. It was so dark I couldn't make out her whole face, but saw her eyes widen through her thick-rimmed glasses. 'Hi, Chris. Who's your friend?'

'This is Brett. He's new at my school', replied Chris. 'Do you want to swap seats and meet him, Fiona?'

Fiona's eyes lit up. 'Sure!'

She grabbed her drink and popcorn and swapped seats with Chris.

No sooner had Chris sat next to Samantha than he started snogging her.

Fiona, the Mystery Girl, moved up one row and sat beside me as the people behind us began to hiss at us angrily. The movie was very gloomy and the theatre was very dark; my new companion could have been a senior citizen for all I knew, as I couldn't make her out. But I immediately started by holding her hand to show I was interested. She held mine tightly; she was keen too. Her hand felt clammy. I was nervous at the thought of pashing someone, so I finally worked up some courage and asked her if I could kiss her. She said yes straight away, and before I knew it, our lips were locked . . . literally. She wore braces.

My lips and tongue were tortured. It was like kissing someone with a mouth full of staples, but I persevered so as not to upset her. We snogged for about five minutes, then took a break to watch the movie for a while, then started up again. Apart from it being like licking a cheese grater, my first real kiss was OK, but I eventually grew bored after about an hour of kissing this mouth full of metal. My youthful urges flew out of the cinema, and I was keen to follow them. I told Fiona I was going to the toilet.

I just kept walking until I reached the bus stop, and went home. Mum, surprised to see me, asked why I was home so early. I lied and said the movie was terrible. I figured it was easier than telling her I had spent the evening with my tongue in a food processor.

3. Playing for the Other Team?

I persevered with trying to be attracted to girls; it seemed to be the expected thing to do. My brothers were always looking at magazines and calendars with pictures of buxom women in sexy bikinis and bringing home a myriad of girlfriends. Chatting up girls and perving on them was all the guys in my class were interested in. I tried my best to do the same, but none of it really pitched my tent. My mind kept sending me mixed messages, and I began to realise I was often looking more at guys. I enjoyed the company of girls . . . but I *really* enjoyed looking at men.

So I had this feeling I might be sexually attracted to guys – and then I watched the TV coverage of the 1976 Summer Olympics, in Montreal, and all those divers in their tiny trunks confirmed my suspicions. I found myself looking more and more at the male models in store catalogues, especially the underwear adverts. My imagination would go into a frenzy every time I looked at record covers with scantily clad glam-rock stars like The Sweet and Queen. It was a weird time. I couldn't really do anything about it, as no one else around me appeared to feel the same.

Those last years at the Catholic high school were one big comedy show. I can't remember ever laughing as hard and as often as I did then. I had girlfriends and mates that were so hilarious my lungs would ache and almost collapse from laughing. We weren't interested in learning at all; we only wanted to joke, laugh and do pranks on teachers and each other. Sister Carson, my science teacher, was probably the most gullible. She had no idea what we used to get up to in class. The science class was set up like a laboratory, with rows of high benches and chairs with sinks, gas jets and Bunsen burners. My friend Ronnie and I would always be the only two sitting in the back row. As soon as we would take our seats, Ronnie would pull his trousers and undies down to his ankles and sit there with a look of serious fascination on his face. Sister Carson would conduct her lesson with no idea that Ronnie was down the back displaying his family jewels. Controlling my laughter was difficult – but not as difficult as trying to control the party going on in my pants.

4. How Embarrassing

I tried to do the right thing and brought some potential girlfriends home to meet the parents. However, my mother was very controlling and was never afraid of making it known to the girls that she didn't really like them; she made sure they got the message loud and clear that no girl would ever be good enough for her precious Brett. No wonder I turned gay. It almost seemed like I didn't have a choice.

I did attempt a relationship with a girl in high school called Deidre. I couldn't resist being with her, because she made me laugh like no other. We were a comedy team. She was pretty, had a fuller figure and was well-fed. Although we spent so much time together, we were never intimate, but I'm sure she would have jumped at the chance had I offered. Well, maybe not 'jumped' – that would have been impossible and painful for us both. Perhaps 'leaned towards my affection'. I brought Deidre home one Saturday afternoon to meet my mum, and I knew it was a mistake the moment we walked inside. Mum was rude and greeted her like she would greet a virus.

'Mum, this is my friend Deidre.'

Mum continued to read her magazine.

Deidre tried. 'Hello, Mrs Preiss – nice to finally meet you.'

Mum looked up from her magazine and stared at the buxom figure in front of her.

My turn. 'Mum, maybe we could have a cup of coffee together?'

Mum threw her magazine on the coffee table and turned her gaze to me, unimpressed.

'Please?' I begged gently.

She gave a heavy, irritated sigh and stood up abruptly, then soldiered on into the kitchen, opened the fridge for the milk, slammed the door, filled the kettle and banged it down on the stove, flung open the cupboards, crashed cups and saucers out onto the table and threw a box of cookies after them.

We sat down meekly at the kitchen table.

Deidre and I tried to make small talk, but Mum clearly wasn't interested. She eventually made the coffees and plonked them in front of us, then rushed outside to hang some washing on the line. Her actions spoke louder than words. Looking at the table, we realised the cookies were 'Limmits', which at that time were well known as diet cookies. Deidre looked at me in disbelief and I glared at Mum through the window. Deidre had no problems opening her mouth wide at the best of times, but I never saw it drop like it did when she saw those diet cookies. She got the hint that Mum didn't like her – and I got the hint that apparently I needed a new girlfriend.

5. Revelation

My last Christmas break before heading to university was mostly spent with my dear friends from the prayer group I had joined the year before. We had a special bond. We sang, prayed and laughed, knowing this could be the last time we would be with each other for years. There were some marathon evenings, staying up together to watch the sunrise.

One of the guys, Peter, was in his early thirties, single, and had spent one or two years studying at a seminary in the hope of becoming a priest. He was a committed Catholic and quite faithful, but eventually felt that becoming a priest wasn't his true calling. Peter told me about his younger brother Simon, a musician in his late twenties; he struggled with light drugs, and his homosexuality was causing a lot of tension with his very religious and conservative parents. Peter had tried for years to talk to Simon; he wanted to help him accept Jesus into his life, clean up, cure his drug addiction – and cure his homosexuality.

Since Simon and I had music in common, Peter wanted me to spend some time talking to him, in the hope of encouraging him to find God. I enjoyed the prayer group – the music, the songs and the chance to get to know God again – but I never thought of myself as a preacher or an evangelist. However, Peter was a dear friend and I wanted to help him out. He took me to Simon's house and introduced me as a friend from the prayer group.

Peter told his brother I was a musician as well, that I played in local bands and had joined the church folk group. We clicked immediately and spoke a lot about our favourite musicians and songs. Simon told me he played guitar and enjoyed writing songs; maybe we could play together one day?

I found Simon extremely attractive. He was handsome, with curly hair and a huge welcoming smile. He was friendly, relaxed . . . and also appeared very interested in me.

Peter excused himself and headed off to do errands, leaving me with my mission to convert Simon. We made coffee. Simon suggested we head to the living room to chat and listen to some Steve Forbert music – he had bought a new album that day. I sat on the sofa, and Simon sat on the floor, rolling his own cannabis and tobacco while listening patiently to me rambling on about music as well as my recent experiences with the prayer group and the church. I did my best to let him see how pure I was. As he lit his joint, I seized the opportunity to tell him I never needed the artificial stimulation of drugs and that being part of a prayer group kept me on the straight and narrow.

Simon remained quiet. He took another couple of drags and blew the smoke slowly out of his mouth and nostrils, nodding his head now and then to acknowledge he was listening. He looked very relaxed and chilled out.

The strong smell had started affecting my mood as well, but I felt proud of myself that this could possibly be my first ever conversion. Jesus was surely smiling down on me.

Simon shuffled along the floor towards me. Just as I was telling him how good Jesus made me feel and how happy I was, he leaned against my knees and started playing gently with the hairs on my ankle. A rush of electricity went through my body and groin. I didn't know how to respond, so I kept rambling on about the prayer group.

Simon's hand slowly moved up my leg. 'Does this bother you?'

All I could do was smile nervously. Simon moved up onto the sofa and sat even closer to me.

I told him that if he embraced Jesus, it might help him address his homosexuality.

He agreed, but decided to embrace me instead.

He kissed me.

I wanted to say, 'Please stop,' but before I knew it, I found myself naked in bed with him saying, 'Please don't stop.'

I wasn't sure if Jesus was still smiling – but I do know that I went home the next morning with a big grin on my face.

Part XX

The Sperm Leaves Home

1. A Taste of Culture

The final year of high school was a real wake-up call. The teachers began the year by giving the students a reality check, reminding us that the effort we put into our last year would equal the kind of job we would get and the kind of life we would have. As I scanned the shabby bunch of teachers I was going to be working with, it was clear they hadn't opened a textbook between them during their own final year of school; their ticket into teaching college was no more than a raffle prize.

In the 1970s, Australia had a shortage of teachers, so a government program was set up to draft unemployed teachers from the USA. Many of them took the opportunity as a way of escaping the draft for Vietnam. They weren't prepared for the hot, dry conditions of outback Australia, and certainly weren't ready to deal with some of the feral students. In hindsight, I'm sure many of those teachers who were tormented by the bullies in my school probably wished they had signed up to fight the Vietcong instead. Mind you, I'm also sure a few of them were asking for it. I knew some were escaping from awful teaching conditions back in the USA, but they were keen as mustard to sign the tax-free contract and treated the adventure to Australia as a temporary exploit. Unfortunately, a lot of them treated the kids the same way.

Mr Burns, who taught us English literature, was from St Louis, Missouri. He was morbidly obese, had a coffee-stained beard and was a chronic stutterer. One day he introduced us to a play called *The Glass Menagerie* by Tennessee Williams, glowing with pride as he announced in his strong southern accent that this famous author also came from his hometown. 'Tennessee Williams is an American playwright and a confirmed homo-homo-homo-homo . . .'

Before he could finally spit out the word, one of the bigmouth bullies, Daniel, shouted at the top of his voice, 'You mean he's a faggot, sir?'

There were a few seconds of shocked silence. Then everyone burst out laughing.

Mr Burns's face suddenly flooded with red and he slammed the book down on the desk, bellowing, 'Y'all hush, now!' Grunting, he refilled his lungs and shouted, 'Daniel! You get yourself out the front here, son, and lick that there chalkboard mighty clean.'

We were stunned. We all hissed, 'What?'

One of the bravest of us, a girl named Marcia, shouted back in Daniel's defence. 'You can't do that, sir! He'll get sick and die!'

Mr Burns, ignoring us all, grabbed Daniel by the scruff of his neck and forced him to lick large sections of chalked handwriting off the board. While he was licking, the rest of us were gagging. When the chalkboard was finally smeared with Daniel's saliva and his tongue was swelling from all the chalk dust, he started spitting and wiping his tongue with his long sleeves. A white tongue and saturated sleeves weren't a good look. He turned to Mr Burns and said, 'I'm going to report you to my parents, sir.'

Burns gulped the final mouthful of coffee sludge from his stained mug, then replied in his soft southern drawl, 'You got parents, son? Well, I'll be darned. In the meantime, you can stand in the trash c-c-c-c-can.'

2. The Caravan

It seemed insane to me that one day of intense exams at the end of the school year would determine the rest of my life; that is the kind of pressure no seventeen-year-old needs. I needed help to cope. It was either drugs, alcohol or God, and I needed every penny I could get to escape to university, so alcohol and drugs were off the list. That left me with giving God another go.

My friend Kathy and I joined a Catholic prayer group with a few fellow students who were mostly our own age. It was lovely. Prayer group kept me off the streets and I made some wonderful, decent friends. We would meet each week at each other's houses. Of course, being a Catholic endeavour, it wasn't entirely without guilt; while everyone else was praying and asking God to help the poor and needy, I was asking Him to help me control my sexual urges. Teenage years are such an awkward, fun, miserable time, and my raging hormones had me masturbating like there was no tomorrow.

Mum and Dad had no idea what I was doing in my final year of high school, as no one in the history of my family had ever attempted higher education; they all left high school after four years to get a job and earn money fast. I insisted on doing the extra two years of school to try to escape to university and widen my horizons, but it meant lots of study. I still shared a bedroom with my younger brother, Trevor, and he complained endlessly to our parents about having to share his personal space with a small group of Christians praying every couple of weeks. He was also annoyed with me studying in the early hours of the morning.

So Dad managed to borrow a caravan from some guy who owed him a huge favour – God only knows what – and plonked it in our backyard, to get me out of the house. Trevor was thrilled, and I loved it. It was another taste of freedom. I did open my books and complete my assignments for the year, but I was too excited to use the caravan as a mere study hub. I saw it as my own party pad, where I could come and go as often and as late as I wanted to. It was the best life; I was far enough away from the house to be on my own, yet close enough to be fed by Mum and have my clothes washed.

Despite this, though, it was the toughest year. I found school and studying a drag, and it was such a hindrance to my social life. I tried to act interested in learning, but finding the discipline to study was arduous. Basically, I couldn't wait for the year to finish so I could leave home and get my ticket to university.

The school sent vocational guidance officers to touch base with all the students regularly, to encourage us to think about what career path we might like to take. I think it was supposed to keep us motivated to study. There was one guidance officer who was visiting from Sydney – a city slicker, very posh and conservative. We sat with her around a table in the library, and we could see immediately she was struggling to understand our outback dialect and rustic choice of words. Ever so politely, she asked, 'So, gentlemen, what would you all like as a career when you leave school?'

'I'd like to be a chippy, Miss.'

'Pardon me – a what?'

'Working with wood, Miss. Making chairs and stuff.'

'I'm sorry. You mean a carpenter?'

'Yeah, that too.'

'OK, that's great. Anybody else?'

'Yeah, me, Miss. I'd like to be a sparkie like me ol' man.'

'A spare key?'

Everyone laughed. 'No, Miss – a sparkie?'

She frowned. 'Is it . . . a fireman?'

We couldn't control ourselves.

'No, Miss. Working with electricity.'

Light – electric or otherwise – dawned. 'Oh! An electrician!'

When it was my turn, I wasn't sure what to say. I had no idea what I really wanted to do, as long as I didn't need to get my hands dirty. So I said, 'I was thinking maybe I would like to be a banker.'

'Lovely. That sounds very creative. Let me find some information for you.'

She proceeded to provide me with a list of the qualifications and certificates I would need. I was expecting to hear what level of math I would need – a knowledge of statistics and so on. However, the things she was saying weren't making any sense to me. Eventually she asked, 'Do you want to work with pastry goods or small goods?'

After some embarrassing silence, it finally dawned on me that she thought I'd said 'baker'. All my mates were cracking up laughing as they caught on as well, but I couldn't be bothered to correct her, so I just said, 'Pastry goods, thanks,' not knowing what the hell they were. I simply let her ramble on about how important it would be for me to start playing with dough and attending cake decorating workshops. I didn't have the heart to tell her I was over baking muffins, cakes and sponges . . . I preferred to eat them instead.

3. The Final Countdown

The last year of high school was ending. I gave all the exams my best shot, but considering the amount of study I hadn't done over the year, I wasn't expecting great results. Maybe not even a pass. In fact, I bought an apron and asked Mum to show me how to make pies, just in case. Getting my hands dirty as a baker might not be such a bad idea after all.

The Christmas holidays came – and so did my exam results. I passed. I couldn't believe it. Maybe there was a God, and maybe He gave me some bonus points for attending those weekly prayer group sessions.

Always included with the exam results was a letter outlining the universities and courses that matched your final score. There were quite a few universities to choose from, but my average results only gave me two choices: I could be either an elementary school teacher or a forest ranger. Coming from the desert, I didn't really have much experience with trees, and in any case I wasn't sure if I was up to being Smokey the Bear and fighting bushfires. The thought of managing campgrounds in national parks didn't appeal to me either; while I'm all for preserving and enjoying nature, I much prefer a five-star hotel. It was pretty clear that studying forestry was not going to happen.

Teaching college, here I come.

My dad was not so keen on me heading to university. Everything came down to money for him, and he was probably having sleepless nights and stressful days worrying I would drain him and Mum of every cent they had just to survive university and gain a teacher's certificate. Now that all the Australian schools were heavily staffed with teachers recruited from the USA, suddenly there was an oversupply. It became national news; Dad was forever cutting out newspaper clippings about it and leaving them on my bed in the caravan. He tried to knock the idea of being a teacher out of my head, constantly proclaiming I would never get a job, and that I should wake up to myself and get a real job in the local mines. Really, Dad? I always wondered what part of 'I don't want a job where I get my hands dirty' he didn't understand. I had my heart set on heading to university. I was going, and nothing was going to stop me. I just needed the money.

We all applied for government scholarships, but it was pure luck who got one – and unfortunately, it wasn't me. I knew I could spend weekends playing in piano bars or bands to get a few dollars, but it would never be enough to pay rent, feed myself, pay for university books . . . Desperate times call for desperate measures, and I was really desperate – to leave town. This was my only chance. One of my dearest friends at the time (who, incidentally, had the gift of making me wet my pants from laughter) had a brother who was a top manager at one of the mines where my dad worked. She was the greatest optimist. She said, 'Go and talk to my brother Jonathan. Maybe the mines might give you a loan to go to university, since your dad works there. He can only say no, but you might get a yes.' I loved that kind of hopeful attitude.

Before I knew it, I was sitting in front of Jonathan in his office, literally begging him to arrange for the mining company to give me a loan to freedom. I promised I would pay it all back once I scored a teaching job somewhere. Jonathan must have been able to see the desperation in my eyes, being a local boy himself who had taken the chance to head out of town, study well and score a managerial position. I guess he could see himself in me, and he knew how friendly I was with his sister. He said, 'Your dad has worked on the mines for over twenty-five years, underground, in appalling conditions. For his service, we will give you the loan, equivalent to the government scholarship and . . . you don't need to pay us back. Consider it a gift. Do well, be a teacher. Don't stay here to be a miner. It's not you, Brett.'

Tears were pouring down my face. I had got a yes. I had got my ticket to university and a chance to be me.

Jonathan hadn't finished speaking. 'We won't tell your dad – he wouldn't understand. Mining is in his blood.'

It was true; mining really was in his blood . . . along with copious amounts of stress hormones and alcohol.

I'm not sure how Dad found out about the money, but I suspect my little brother told him. I think Trevor might have heard me shouting it out in my sleep one night, as I was constantly dreaming of my exciting future. Anyhow, he told me Dad found out and had tried to stop the mines from paying me because he considered it a waste of money; he suspected the teaching was a cover story and I was really going to a seminary to become a priest!

I thought this was an ironic response, given that half his life's wages – the half he didn't spend on destroying his liver – were spent on putting four boys through an expensive Catholic education. Surely Dad had considered the possibility that subjecting our young minds to eleven years of Catholic indoctrination might result in one of us being radicalised and receiving the 'calling' to the cloth? I have to admit that joining the priesthood did cross my mind at one point, but upon closer examination of the fleeting thought, I realised it wasn't so much a desire to become a priest, but more of a fantasy of sleeping with one . . . which I did, as an adult. All those points I'd accumulated from God for attending the prayer groups regularly were wiped clean (along with my penis) after I copulated with the clergy.

Fortunately, Dad didn't succeed in cancelling my funds and lived long enough to see me graduate as a teacher – evidence that I didn't use the mining kitty to become a priest. He must have had some very restless nights during those university years. My good friend Kathy was fortunate to get a scholarship and was able to reject the forestry course as well; we both chose the same teaching course at a university in a place called Lismore, on the north-east coast of Australia. I had never heard of it, but going so far away sounded exciting, and being on the coast would be a bonus. I'd suffered more than my fair share of desert heat and dust storms. It was time to catch a mouthful of waves.

I spent most of the summer Christmas break packing and having farewell parties. Mum was packing as well. She said she needed a little holiday adventure, but I suspected she wasn't coping with the thought of finally having to cut the umbilical cord with me. I didn't mind. I wanted her to see where I would be living for the next few years – and besides, I needed her to give me a crash course in survival cooking, using a washing machine, making a bed – all the things she had spent years doing ad infinitum for her troop of monkeys. It was embarrassing, really; none of my brothers, myself nor Dad had ever touched the washing machine, made a bed, or cooked a decent meal. We wouldn't have survived without Mum.

In fact, the very few times I recall her being sick in bed for a week, either with a virus or from sheer exhaustion, the household shut down completely. Suddenly, the social structure and behaviour of all her offspring and the big baboon of a husband changed. Dominance, competition and aggressive raids suddenly flew out the window and the five primates sat staring at each other, sucking their thumbs, wondering which of them might be able to boil an egg.

Instead of scheming and marking our territories, we found ourselves making short-term alliances, bonding and grooming each other in the hope that someone's cooking gene would kick in so we didn't have to eat each other into extinction. I had the upper hand during this brief maternal shutdown; I could, in fact, boil an egg, so this was the menu for every meal. But the other monkeys soon got sick of it and quickly abandoned the zoo – and their mother.

Not an ounce of compassion was in their blood, and not for one moment did they consider staying to help Mum with cleaning the house or even to make her a cup of tea. The mongrels just fled to their friends' houses to bludge off their families for a few days. I stayed, did what I could do to help Mum feel more comfortable – and mastered the art of boiling an egg.

4. *New Year's Eve*

I felt as if I were leaving home forever. Much to my mother's dismay, I packed absolutely everything, including my guitar, electric piano, amplifier and all the sheets of music I had accumulated over the years. As Kathy and I were travelling to Lismore by train, it was a good thing that the cost of transporting massive amounts of luggage was cheap in those days. It was a twenty-four-hour train trip to university, so there wouldn't be many opportunities to zip back home to collect anything. I needed to take everything, and there was enough to fill a train carriage.

With a few weeks left before we embarked on our new adventure, Kathy decided to hold a combined farewell and New Year's Eve party at her house because her parents were going to be away for a few days. It was a fancy-dress party, and everyone brought their own drinks. I decided to go as a Roman, using an old sheet as a toga. However, I needed a tan. Kathy and I decided to spend every day for two weeks at the local swimming pool, sunbaking in the scorching heat. We covered our bodies with apricot kernel oil and basically cooked ourselves. We ended up as brown as coffee and looked stunning in our togas, glowing like bronze statues. However, thirty years later, I found myself glowing like a baker's oven from all the laser treatment at the skin cancer clinic, removing carcinoma and my sun-damaged skin. That apricot kernel oil tan made me look healthy and sexy. Now I have a face like a fingerprint.

The New Year's Eve party was a blast – one of the best parties I had ever been to, and a great way to say farewell to friends and celebrate the new chapter we were about to embark upon. Kathy and I had done loads of preparation, making cupcakes, nibbles and a strong punch. There were balloons and streamers everywhere, and we had all the records ready to go, in alphabetical order from ABBA to Ziggy Stardust. The party was meant to be for close friends, but as with any party in Broken Hill, once the word got around or someone could smell 'party' in the air, it became an open invitation. People would follow their noses, gatecrash and make it their own. We had no idea who we were drinking and dancing with, or who we were snogging during the midnight kiss. We didn't care. We were merely getting drunk and having the party of a lifetime.

Some strange things happened that remain forever etched on my mind. I remember someone accidentally lit the backyard on fire with a cigarette butt and rushed into the house shouting, 'Kathy, your backyard is on fire!' Kathy was so drunk and so busy grooving to the Bay City Rollers music blasting out in the living room that she just shouted, 'Let the bastard burn!' and continued bopping to her favourite band. Someone else suffered from cupcake phobia and was stealthily squashing them into the kitchen floor. We never caught them, and we were too inebriated to think of checking everyone's shoes. At one point I headed out to the front yard with my drink, to get some fresh air, and saw a guy standing on the brick fence with his pants around his ankles, pissing into Kathy's letterbox (I later heard he'd done more than that, but I didn't have the stomach to check). However, I learnt at that moment never ever to host an open-invitation party – or become a postman.

The big day came. Kathy and I were finally standing on

the train station platform, with all our friends there to send us off. Both our mothers were already seated on the train, ready for the big journey to the coast. We made the most of our last minutes together with our dear friends, hugging and kissing everyone, singing our favourite prayer group hymns and shedding tears.

Boarding the train, it dawned on us that the chapter of our lives set in this dusty outback mining town was finally over. Nothing would ever be the same again. And all those special dear friends waving us goodbye – the people who had shared years of good times and bad, and given us the sweetest memories – would disperse as well to begin their own life journeys. Watching them fade away as the long train slowly departed was too much to bear. Kathy and I hugged each other tightly; we bawled our eyes out for ages. I was a mess. I wasn't sure if my tears were a wave of sadness from leaving my dear friends or the painful joy a person feels after being released from prison. Perhaps they were both.

As the long train snaked its way through the desert towards the east coast, I curled up in my seat, hugging a pillow and staring out of the window. It was almost as if I were that sperm again, beginning its journey, one of many passengers heading to an unknown destination. I really had no idea what to expect, but instinctively, I knew this was my destiny; there was an unexplained force compelling me to keep going, to explore and conceive a future life. This time I was really on my own and I had to stay afloat, fight the current and struggle against the tides, no matter what.

I knew I could do it. As that me-sperm survived the chaos in the vagina and made it to the finish line, I had survived my bizarre childhood and finally made it to the rail line. I had my ticket to freedom, and my life at university would now be in the hands of Mr Fate. I wondered whether the next phase of my life would be ordinary, or even more bizarre.

Bring it on.

I was off like a bride's nightie.

ABOUT THE AUTHOR

Brett Preiss was born in a mining town in the hot, dry outback of Australia. With itchy feet and longing for sea air, he headed to the tropical east coast. It was the perfect place to go to university, surf, and eat his first mango. When he discovered there was a world beyond Down Under, he packed his bags, and for the next thirty years taught internationally in Japan, Germany and the Netherlands.

He is an author, ESL teacher, musician and mindfulness instructor. He also loves to tell jokes and tap dance (not at the same time!). Before diving into the rich material his life provides, Brett entered the writing foray with his first book, *Go, Percy! Go!*, which was published in English and then in Dutch as *Hup, Peter! Hup!* His second book, *I'm Crazy About Holland Because . . .* , was a chance to share his love for cows, cheese and clogs. He enjoys creating resources for educators, as well as writing fiction for children and adults.

One of his favourite quotes is from an English author, Humphrey Carpenter: *'The nice thing about being a writer is that you can make magic happen without learning tricks'*.

Acknowledgements

Special thanks are given to those who helped make this book possible:

Beacon Point LLC for editing.

Robin J Samuels at Shadowcat Editing for proofreading.

Cutting Edge Studios/Black Bee Media for cover design, formatting and publishing support.

The SPS Community for all their help and guidance.

Jos van de Water for for his endless optimism and support.

Self-Publishing School

NOW IT'S YOUR TURN

Discover the EXACT 3-step blueprint you need to become a bestselling author in as little as 3 months.

Self-Publishing School helped me, and now I want them to help you with this FREE resource to begin outlining your book!

Even if you're busy, bad at writing, or don't know where to start, you CAN write a bestseller and build your best life.

With tools and experience across a variety of niches and professions, Self-Publishing School is the only resource you need to take your book to the finish line!

DON'T WAIT

Say "YES" to becoming a bestseller:

https://self-publishingschool.com/friend/

Follow the steps on the page to get a FREE resource to get started on your book and unlock a discount to get started with Self-Publishing School

Thank You For Reading My Book!

I really appreciate all of your feedback, and I love hearing what you have to say.

Please leave me an honest review on Amazon letting me know what you thought of the book.

Thanks so much!

Brett Preiss

Manufactured by Amazon.ca
Bolton, ON